I AN DISTRACTED BY ƎVERYTHING

AN ANNUAL FOR GROWN-UPS

LIZA TARBUCK

MICHAEL JOSEPH

an imprint of

PENGUIN BOOKS

MICHAEL JOSEPH

UK | USA | Canada | Ireland | Australia
India | New Zealand | South Africa

Michael Joseph is part of the Penguin Random House group of companies whose
addresses can be found at global.penguinrandomhouse.com.

First published 2017
001

Design by Liza Tarbuck and Jon Whitelocke

Colour reproduction by Altaimage Ltd

Printed in Germany, by Firmengruppe APPL, aprinta druck, Wemding

A CIP catalogue record for this book is available from the British Library

ISBN: 978-0-718-18378-3

Penguin Random House is committed to a
sustainable future for our buisness, our readers
and our planet. This book is made from Forest
Stewardship Council® certified paper

i hope you find something in here that tickles your fancy.

I consider my love of distraction a thing to be cherished, it nourishes my curiosity so new ideas can blossom, and this book is designed to be an easy companion for others like me, who enjoy a mental ramble.

I loved an annual in my youth (*Bert Fegg's Nasty Book for Boys and Girls*) because I could continue to revisit it and get reabsorbed in the content. So when it came to writing my first book, I knew this was a format that would suit the way I think, however loose my interpretation might be.

Nothing in the questions or puzzles requires an internet enquiry: they're easily figured out, or you could take the query to a mate, and talk.

The pictures may prompt you to recall or feel something. They may not.

I've used some of the texts and emails I get on my Radio 2 show because I think they're funny, and I enjoy the social observations in them, the phrasing of words. They meld me to people I don't actually know, and together we bulge.

This isn't an autobiography in the traditional sense, but it is full of curated personal history; we'll have a lot to talk about when we bump into each other.

Everything in this book has genuinely distracted me.

We're in this together.

liza

All the answers are in your hands.

You may not *like* everything you read. Certain attitudes may at times infuriate you, or the opinion or approach of the writer to his subject run contrary to yours. But one thing is certain; once started on a piece you will be carried along, willy-nilly, to the finish.

In this book you are given a passage to adventure and exploration in two worlds, the physical and the spiritual, from which you will return refreshed, broadened and perhaps even not quite the same person who embarked upon the trip.

You will also, before you are done, have encountered yourself on this voyage and learned something of the marvellous secrets of your own body and senses and the mysterious storage vaults of the subconscious. And finally, even before you have reached the end, you may likewise have discovered hitherto unrevealed and unsuspected areas of warmth and sympathy for your fellows awakened in the recesses of your own human heart.

PAUL GALLICO

Things in my house that stare at me...

HOLY CROSS CONVENT PREPARATORY SCHOOL

KINGSTON

IN CRUCE SALUS

REPORT

on _Lisa Tarbuck_

from _May 8th_ to _July 17th_

Class _Prep. 2_   Average Age _9 yrs. 5 mths_

REMARKS

Lisa has worked quite well during the term. She could, however, do better if she were not so easily distracted. The general appearance of quite good worked is spoiled by untidy presentation.

Lisa is always cheerful, usually obedient and most willing to help. She is kind to the other children and generally is popular in class.

T. Mc Envoy.

School re-opens _Sept. 11th_

Date _July 17th._

Sr. Dominic
HEADMISTRESS

SBS P2806

who
is hiding the fruit?

Sr Anna   Sr Bridget   Sr Corinna   Sr Dearbhla   Sr Eva   Sr Fidelma

Once took some black pudding out of the freezer only to find a defrosted mole! I had found it in the garden and intended to send it to Chris Packham for *Springwatch*. Incidentally, I did send something frozen to Chris Packham once. I found a dead green woodpecker, froze it and then sent it in a jiffy bag. Fools in the production office didn't open it quickly enough and I was blamed for the awful smell.

MRS D

My mum and I once watched my dad going through a bag full of duty free and magazines at Manchester airport in an attempt to find his newspaper. 'Where's the paper?' he asked. 'In your bag' my mum told him. He'd been rooting through the bag of a young couple sitting opposite us. The look on their faces was a picture.

JANE – WAKEFIELD

Was once walking to work and a squirrel fell from a tree and landed on my head. In a moment of sheer panic I started to run about screaming, trying to remove the rodent from my head. This was much to the amusement of a dozen parents dropping off their kids at the local primary school.

CHRIS – DARLINGTON

New word: 'Petrichor'. The dusty smell after rain.

FIONA – EDINBURGH

My iPad keeps changing my husband's name Stephen to Sparkles.

JANE – ROCHDALE

Sign language alphabet

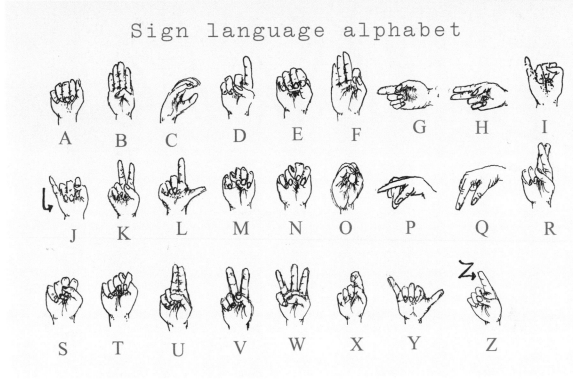

A B C D E F G H I
J K L M N O P Q R
S T U V W X Y Z

why would you be knotting about a supermarket?

Ten French words or phrases that are used everyday... ALLEZ

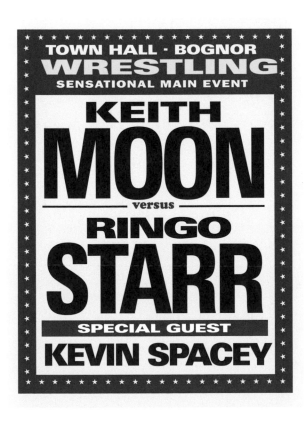

TOWN HALL · BOGNOR
WRESTLING
SENSATIONAL MAIN EVENT
KEITH
MOON
versus
RINGO
STARR
SPECIAL GUEST
KEVIN SPACEY

Taut Thriller Dennis Waterman stars as 'The Bloody Queen'

How many words describe the swapping of information, chatter, gossip, espionage, shouting, interrogation dancing. oh god it's a pandora's box... & words don't even cover it because then there's the picture they're conjured...

it's clearly no accident that nostrils are finger sized is it?

Gall Oak Ink

Acorns have long held our fascination, their symbolism is a clue to the reverence of past generations; a doorway to potential, strength and new beginnings, fertility, spiritual pathways and protection. Pagan celebrations often include the oak, particularly at solstices and equinoxes, contact with the tree providing deep-rooted security with nature, intuitively speaking for things that have no words, a tree and its fruit as a separate language.

Used in the past in place of grains, acorns can be arduous to prepare for human use because of the need to expel bitter tannins, but they are high in proteins, fats, carbohydrates and various vitamins and minerals.

The clever Gall Wasp knows that by laying her eggs in an acorn, it will nourish her larvae, and in turn this little insect's secretions will transform the acorn into another facility, the oak gall.

The oak gall has played a fundamental part in our understanding of the past, because without its ink, important documents simply wouldn't exist. The earliest examples we have date from around the 4th century, and move forward to include all aspects of human life, from secular to civic, the arts, sciences and the everyday.

Its water resistance has proved invaluable, and when used on parchment, it can only be rubbed out by scratching, useful if you travel by water or hold any anxiety that a document may be tampered with.

To make yourself some ink you will need:
- A solution of iron sulphate.
- Some oak galls. Go for darker ones - if they've got holes in them, that's good, the insect has left!
- Gum arabic, optional. It works as a binder and adds viscosity to the finished product, art supply shops usually have it, but it's not essential if you're only messing around.

The amounts you use are trial and error really, depending on what you're using the ink for.

Crush the galls and leave them to soak in water overnight. *(Sir Isaac Newton soaked his in strong ale for a month!)*

Mix the iron sulphate with a little water and add to the crushed oak galls.

You have the option of leaving this mixture to mingle for as long as you can, but if you're impatient to try it...

Filter it through an old tight or similar to get the bits out.

This is where you'd add a little bit of gum arabic - it's water soluble.

It'll be quite light initially, but will darken over time.

Store it in an airtight jar because it's quick to oxidize, but you can always add a bit of water to refresh.

The acidity of the ink can destroy metals, so when capillary action fountain pens became all the rage in the early 20th Century, the recipes for ink had to be reinvented.

You may now want to make yourself a quill... in for a penny and all that.

This ink can cause documents to deteriorate over time, an increasing problem for our conservationists.

Yellow
Orange
Red
Pink

Purple
Blue
Light Green
Dark Green

AMBERGRIS

Inside a sperm whale, the build-up of fish bones and squiddy bits from various meals would cause a problem, if the whale's intelligent digestive system didn't have a solution. It forms a waxy substance to surround the bony mass and the whale can then eject it, rather like a fur ball.

This bolus floats about on the ocean's currents, subjected to sun and salt, and with time, transforms into ambergris.

It may look like a rock, but it's very light and waxy to touch, and when added to perfume it acts like a fixative. It tethers all the different components together and allows the scent to last a long time.

It's highly prized by the perfume trade and, as it's so rare, very valuable.

How the hell did they ever know what to do with it in the first place? Amazing.

I'd like to feel some.

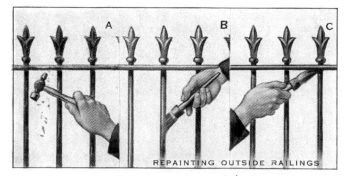

REPAINTING OUTSIDE RAILINGS

'grief pounded me like waves.'
The Goldfinch D.T.

Awful, how even subliminal, but I bet someone thought themselves very clever indeed.

my brother telling me that when your mouse arrow flies across your computer screen, someone has just entered your computer...

WHY DOES A BISHOP carry a crook? *

BARGE).
Braille (brah-ē), Louis (1809–52). French inventor, himself blind, of the *Braille* (brāl) *system* of printing for the blind; it consists

A	B	C	D	E	F	G	H
I	J	K	L	M	N	O	P
Q	R	S	T	U	V		X
Y	Z	and	for	of	the		W

BRAILLE CHARACTERS

TAKING CUTTINGS

RIGHT WAY WRONG WAY

I love it when a worker arrives at your home and you catch a whiff of fabric conditioner. Somebody adores this person. They want their clothes to be soft and clean and that's nicely fussy. Chances are, they're going to do you a lovely job.

SEE IT LIVE ★ REAL STARS
WRESTLING
★ JIMMY ★
CARR
★★★ VERSUS ★★★
★ HUGH ★
LAURIE
SPECIAL GUEST
MINNIE DRIVER

* To get to the other side.

STAR TREK

The most popular cult TV series of all time...

UNIFORM COLOURS INDICATED THE ROLE OF THE CREW MEMBER: GOLD - COMMAND ROUTE, BLUE - SCIENCE DEPARTMENTS, RED - SUPPORT SERVICES

Chekov - *Walter Koenig*
Walter Koenig played Pavel Chekov... The Monkees were taking the US by storm and Walter had a look of Davy Jones about him. This was played up by the studio and they paid special attention to his hair, attempting a mop top style.

Scotty - *James Doohan*
Chief engineer Montgomery Scott, played by WW2 hero James Doohan. Scotty's unbending responsibility for the ship's good health created a kind of mythology around the USS Enterprise that made the ship feel like another character in her own right. Scotty was an inspiration for many to take up engineering as a career. His middle finger was shot off during the D-Day landings.

Captain James T Kirk - *William Shatner*
Played with energy and determination by William Shatner. Unpredictable and romantic, with a great sense of fun, all of omankind had a bit of a thing for Kirk, but e had important bold man stuff to do, and nothing came between him and his ship.

STAR TREK CREATOR GENE RODDENBURY BELIEVED THERE WAS NO CHEST HAIR IN THE FUTURE - AND THAT'S WHY SHATNER HAD TO BE SHAVED BY A STUDIO BARBER WHEN HE WAS APPEARING TOPLESS

Spock - *Leonard Nimoy*
Leonard Nimoy's commitment to playing the unemotional Spock was a part of the whole show's magic. Among his contributions was Spock's iconic hand gesture 'live long and prosper'. . . it's based on the blessing that Cohanim priests give to their congregation.

TELEPORTATION (BEAM ME UP) WAS USED TO NEGATE THE NEED FOR SHOTS OF SPACESHIPS LANDING WHICH WOULD BE TOO EXPENSIVE IN TIME

Lt. Hikaru Sulu - *George Takei, Helmsman*
Sulu's easy intelligence and focus made him a vital part of the crew. Sulu and Chekhov set the bar high for what side-by-side teamwork could achieve.

THE FIRST INTERRACIAL KISS ON TV (KIRK AND UHURA) WAS ACTUALLY MEANT TO BE BETWEEN UHURA AND SPOCK

Nurse Chapel - *Majel Barrett*
Majel Barrett was originally cast as 'Number One' (first officer) but TV execs decided that audiences would have a problem with a woman being in a position of power. Majel voiced all the onboard computers and also played Nurse Christine Chapel.
She was married to Gene Roddenberry.

Dr 'Bones' McCoy - *DeForest Kelley*
Kelley's cannon of acting roles include a vast array of cowboys and villains prior to joining Star Trek. He was originally offered the role of Spock, which he refused.

Expendable Crew Member
This is the guy who's never been seen before and suddenly he's in the gang. He gets killed to heighten the danger the central crew are in.

LUCILLE BALL SINGLE-HANDEDLY STOPPED STAR TREK BEING CANCELLED IN ITS FIRST SERIES: SHE WAS HEAD OF THE PRODUCTION COMPANY DESILA WHO MADE IT

I LOVED EVERYTHING ABOUT THE SHOW, THE CONTAINED WORLD OF THE SHIP, THE CONTRAST OF OTHER PLANETS, THE OUTFITS AND HAIR, THE COLOUR...I LOVED THE CAMARADERIE AND SATISFYING FEEL - GOOD ENDINGS...LEADING-EDGE ENTERTAINMENT TO MY GENERATION...

DOUGAL

I could've watched him for hours, I loved him I think

it's why I went on to adore Robert Dougall the Newsreader... "What's in a name? That which we call a rose By any other name would smell as sweet."

PLAN OF WORK FOR A SMALL SERVANTLESS HOUSE
(3 or 4 in family)

Time	Morning	Time	Afternoon / Evening
7.0.	Get up ; dress.	2.0.	Wash up, tidy kitchen and scullery.
10.	Strip the bed and air the rooms.	10.	
20.	Unlock the house.	20.	
30.	Stoke the boiler.	30.	
40.	Light living-room fire if necessary.	40.	
50.	Prepare breakfast.	50.	Change.
8.0.	Have breakfast.	3.0.	
10.		10.	
20.	Clear away, wash up breakfast things. (Accompany child to school when required.)	20.	Recreation, resting, visiting or special duties such as ironing, gardening, needlework according to weather and season. Minding young children if necessary.
30.		30.	
40.		40.	
50.		50.	
9.0.	Sweep porch and steps.	4.0.	
10.	Lay sitting-room fire if needed.	10.	
20.	Do dining-room and sitting-room carpets with vacuum cleaner. Mop the surrounds and dust.	20.	
30.		30.	
40.		40.	Prepare and serve tea.
50.		50.	
10.0.	Make beds.	5.0.	
10.	Mop and dust upstair rooms and W.C.	10.	Wash up tea things.
20.	Attend to bathroom. Wash out bath and lavatory basin. Sweep and mop bathroom floor and landing. Sweep stairs.	20.	
30.		30.	
40.		40.	
50.		50.	
11.0.	Look over larder.	6.0.	Prepare food for supper or dinner, and cook the meal.
10.	Prepare vegetables or pastry for midday or evening meal.	10.	
20.		20.	
30.		30.	
40.		40.	
50.		50.	
	Shopping when required and special weekly duties.	7.0.	Put children to bed.
12.0.		10.	
10.		20.	
20.		30.	
30.		40.	Serve and have dinner.
40.	Finish off cooking, and prepare lunch.	50.	
50.			
1.0.	Serve lunch or dinner.	8.0.	Clear away meal. Wash up if liked, but this can be deferred until the morning.
10.		10.	
20.	Have lunch, and clear away.	20.	
30.		30.	
40.		40.	Reading, recreation, letter writing, accounts.
50.		50.	

As meal-times vary considerably in different families and in different parts of the country, according to the nature of the husband's work the principal meal is sometimes taken in the middle and sometimes at the end of the day. As a general rule, when the husband's work is near at hand and he can take all meals at home, the principal meal is taken at midday, and the housewife's morning will be necessarily busier, but she should have more leisure between tea and supper.

HOUSEWIFE'S WEEKLY DUTIES
From 11.30 to 12.30

MONDAY.	Brush all clothes used over the week-end and put away. Collect large articles and send to laundry or do laundrywork at home. If all family laundry is done at home, help may be necessary. Wash silk and woollens first, followed by white things. These can be done in alternate weeks if preferred.
TUESDAY.	Turn out dining-room. Clean silver.
WEDNESDAY.	Special turning out of two bedrooms each week.
THURSDAY.	Special turning out of sitting-room.
FRIDAY.	Thorough weekly clean of bathroom, W.C., landing and stairs. Baking.
SATURDAY.	Special cleaning of hall, kitchen and scullery. Extra cooking for week-end.

THERE ARE SEVERAL THINGS TO CONSIDER WHEN I PICK THE PLAYLISTS FOR MY SHOW.

I'm playing to a broad spectrum of people: every age, all manner of opinion and any amount of musical taste.

The timings are crucial. It's the norm to play between eight and ten tracks in any hour, & I try and get twelve away, but plan for fifteen. - *gives us a bit of leeway*

An opening song should change your palate from the previous show and hint at what's to come. If I get the opening track right, the rest just flows.

The time of the show is crucial; what are people doing while they're listening & what would I want to listen to in their position?

I like to assemble the tracks so one somehow fits with the next & works as a continuous hour as if there were no talking in between.

Music changes energy.

I can't bear a trite lyric: sometimes this can be overlooked, but rarely.

The length of a song is important, anything over four minutes has to tick a lot of boxes before I'll put it in.

'Silly' is a good thing in moderation.

I'm not a fan of computerised drums, likewise an organ can lose its appeal within minutes, but there are exceptions.

Some older songs may be offensive to someone listening and unless there's a tongue-in-cheek element to them, they don't get in.

I love a purist & will hunt definitive music down on the premise the appeal could stretch and inform. Difficult tracks are often aided by what you put before and after them, or setting them up with interesting notes.

The seasons play their part too. *As does the time the show goes out, we need different things from the radio at different times of the day or night, some music doesn't feel right... ✳*

✳ This could be cobblers though, 'listen again' & all that

There are people whose musical taste I admire unquestioningly and I love it when they tip me off.

I like a memory jog.

I'm allowed (my rule) to play some of my favourite tunes a few times a year, listening to them on the BBC studio equipment can take my breath away. It's part of the reason I do the show.

I listen to what's playing everywhere I go. How does it makes me feel? Shops have people whose job it is to keep you in there with a good soundtrack.

Playing 'The Stripper' makes me laugh; somebody somewhere has an adventure because that track has come on.

I'm mindful of the shows that follow mine and I can lay a foundation for them to wet the listeners' whistle...similarly I like to end on a high – it's helpful for the following show.

Moaning people are rarely helpful & I avoid them when I can. I am always allowed to moan.

You either 'get it' or you don't. Worrying about dissent only waters the product down; I'm a hard taskmaster, I take my job seriously, and as a creative, detail is key.

I consider it an honour to have my own show on BBC radio.

If the music is good the rest of the show takes care of itself. *80% of a live show is about how it's received by the listeners on the day, you have to guess or steer unknown moods. I don't always get it right.*

You gotta have soul.

remastered tracks from the 90's are often quite flat – I tend to avoid them.

Sometimes the musicians are so involved in a song it gives the music an emotional life, ensuring its longevity.

Some weeks I'm so excited by a track I can't wait to play it & guage the reaction.

I'm mindful that I'm imposing my taste on people, but it's lucky that music is so enjoyable... mixing it up's good.

Sometimes I reply to one song with another, personal sport.

He's shouting for his mates, but only the neighbours can hear him ...

DRESS UP
ALAN

DIANA DORS

My husband tried to remove a small conifer from the front garden. Rather than use the correct tools (or employ a professional), he decided to tie it to the tow bar of his car, revved her up, and pulled it up by the roots. Fabulous success. Right up until it ploughed through the back windscreen.

IORNA

My lovely dad Pete did such a big sneeze that it set off the house alarm.

AJ

I found a 15cm goldfish on our trampoline earlier this week. It was still alive! I shouted in German to our neighbour from our attic window (in our normally quiet village) *'Ich habe ein Goldfisch gefunden!'* Our neighbour was wondering where it had gone.

ALAN & SUSAN – BASEL

My wife gets upset when they read out the attendance at a football match and it's an odd number. She thinks someone has gone by themselves.

STEVE – ANDOVER

My wife's mad family have named their ancient cooler box Jerome. Jerome comes on every holiday and even has his own seat in the car. He is treated with more respect than me.

DAVID – CHESLYN HAY

Help the man on the couch by pointing out all the tools and items that he claims he cannot find to get his house in order. There are 16 items altogether:

These lists are a selection, randomly picked from my R2 show from the last 3 years. Do I think they're all good? NO, but they're good company, & may promote memories or dancing... They are always carefully placed so they could be played back to back with no stupid talking... but I'm not allowed... if there is a perfect segue/seague we don't resist it... These are first hours, bit safer than second hr. ♥ I LOVE music ♥

1959? **Bonanza** Lorne Greene
I love Lorne G. he tells a good tale & he means it. The whole cowboys & indians thing is of its time & conjures different things for everyone. Horse riding rythmn to open the show is good for 2 mins.

Jealousy Billy Fury
Drama, carries the momentum an... "wondrous place" is my fave Billy Fury track though...

Come On Eileen Dexy's Midnight Runners
good to welcome an old friend actually softens it... Linda Green memory for me

1967/8 **Cinderella Rockerfella** Esther & Abi Ofarim
Nostalgic track, mums mate Pat ran pubs & this reminds me of her so it must've been on the juke box

Love is the Drug Roxy Music
serious bass, I love this for a myriad of reasons, classic...

♥ **Be Thankful For What You've Got** William De Vaughn
oh how I Love this... got a bit of everything
♥

Get Back The Beatles
reworked protest song, another great 'driver'

Rave On M.Ward
love this fella & this is a beautifully thought out cover

I Think I Love You The Partridge Family
Nostalgia, drama,

She's in Fashion Suede
Classic. effortlessly good on the ear, feels summery & its era

Can't Get Used to Losing You The Beat
rude boy icon .. 'The Harder they come' Album was a game changer for me

linked by Saxa to ↓
007 (Shanty Town) Desmond Decker

Something Tells Me Cilla Black
2:30
fresh & easy & its Cilla! End of the hour means it may not get played if we're inundated with texts & emails, but this reminds me of summer shows with Cilla & dad, watching from the wings. I loved her & Bobby.

Great "pop" **Lollipop** The Mudlarks
Great ender, under 2 mins, fun & familiar

♥ **The Pink Panther Theme** Henry Mancini
Instrumental masterpiece. I imagine certain tracks make people dance or more or interpret... especially if you're on your own. Lovely ender if needed

My partner and I frequently walk past a square jelly cube stuck to the wall opposite a church in Hereford town centre that's been there for years and years, gently decaying. Means we're on the way to Tesco's for shopping.

CHRIS AND RIA – HEREFORD

When we were little and had two grandmas, we used to differentiate them by their dog's name. So 'Grandma Sherry' and 'Grandma Kim'; when Sherry died my Grandma became known as 'Grandma No-Dog'.

LILY – LIVERPOOL

My new word is 'lalochezia'. It means the emotional relief gained from using profane or abusive language.

SINEAD – MANCHESTER.

I once phoned a local Chinese takeaway, placed an order, and went to collect it. When I got home I realized it was all wrong and I called the takeaway to complain. I soon discovered that I had collected a takeaway from an entirely different establishment.

MARTIN

My husband Norman picked up the wrong suitcase at Zurich airport at the start of our skiing holiday. Instead of having my posh Gucci shoes which I had packed for our grand gala evening, I found some crumpled clothes, a bottle of whiskey and a bag of bagels. We had rather a large row.

KIM – BARNET

PLAN OF WORK FOR MISTRESS AND ONE HELPER

Kitchen, Scullery, Dining-room, Sitting-room, and 4 Bedrooms

HOUSEWIFE'S DAILY DUTIES

Time	Duty	Time	Duty
7.0. 10. 20. 30. 40. 50.	Get up and open bed. If there are children, help them to dress; bath and dress baby, as this is likely to ensure a peaceful breakfast. Cook breakfast, if helper is not resident.	2.0. 10. 20. 30. 40. 50.	Help with clearing away and tidying when there are several in family. Look after children when necessary.
8.0. 10. 20. 30. 40. 50.	Have breakfast. Take children to school if necessary.	3.0. 10. 20. 30. 40. 50.	Free for visiting, receiving friends, social work, sewing, gardening, preserve making, amusements, or supervising the children.
9.0. 10. 20. 30. 40. 50.	Make beds and tidy bedrooms. Mop floor and dust.	4.0. 10. 20. 30. 40. 50.	Tea.
10.0. 10. 20. 30. 40. 50. 11.0. 10. 20. 30. 40. 50.	Special weekly work, such as preparing sitting-rooms or bedrooms for the helper to turn out. Washing smalls, ironing, using vacuum cleaner, household sewing, special silver cleaning, etc.	5.0. 10. 20. 30. 40. 50.	Looking after baby or supervising children's studies.
12.0. 10. 20. 30. 40. 50.	Shopping when required or taking the baby out. Cooking or supervising the lunch.	6.0. 10. 20. 30. 40. 50.	Supervising or cooking of dinner or supper when necessary.
1.0. 10. 20. 30. 40. 50.	Have lunch.	7.0. 10. 20. 30. 40. 50.	Have supper or dinner.
		8.0.	Clear away supper if daily helper only is kept. Reading, recreation, letter writing, accounts from 8.40 onwards.

HOUSEWIFE'S WEEKLY DUTIES

From 11.30 to 12.30.

MONDAY. Brush all clothes used over the week-end and put away. Collect large articles and send to laundry or do laundrywork at home. If all family laundry is done at home, help may be necessary.
Wash silk and woollens, followed by white things. These can be done alternate weeks if preferred.

TUESDAY. Help turn out dining-room. Clean silver.

WEDNESDAY. Special turning out of one or two bedrooms each week.

THURSDAY. Special turning out of sitting-room.

FRIDAY. Thorough weekly clean of bathroom, W.C., landing and stairs. Baking for the week-end.

SATURDAY. Special cleaning of hall, kitchen and scullery. Extra cooking for week-end.

Memory game ahead
On the next pages are
30 objects. Look at
them for 1 minute,
close the book and try
to remember as many
as you can.

MERRY CHRISTMAS
GLAD NEW YEAR
FROM
ME TO YOU

MY PRECIOUS DEAR

THE OLD LIGHTHOUSE
DUNGENESS

ADULT
21671

ST. MAUR'S LACROSSE TOUR, U.S.A. 1982

*W*omen in *song*

Love has been woven into music since the first whistleblower took his hollowed-out bone into the woods and blew. Lyrics take the sentiment of a melody into shared emotional participation and here are some women who have inspired unforgettable love songs.

Pattie Boyd

'**Something**' George Harrison 1969
'**Layla**' Eric Clapton 1970
'**Wonderful Tonight**' Eric Clapton 1976

Pattie was already a jobbing model when she was cast as a schoolgirl in the Beatles film 'A Hard Day's Night'. George Harrison was smitten by her from the off, he asked Pattie out, and after much tooing and froing, they become an item. They were eventually engaged on Christmas Day 1965, and married a month later.

To be in the dizzying midst of Beatlemania and an active participant in the expanding nature of the 1960s must've been both overwhelming and fantastic, and Pattie was exploring mysticism via Transcendental Meditation. She was pivotal in introducing the Fab Four and their tribe into this avenue of the search for the meaning of life.

George wrote the song 'Something' for her, which was covered by a multitude of great musicians.

George's favourite version was by James Brown.

Eric Clapton, George Harrison's best friend, fell in love with Mrs Harrison, writing 'Layla' about her. The song was inspired by the fifth-century Arabian tale of impossible love, 'The Story of Layla and Majnun', and whilst Pattie very firmly stayed married, the following years with George became increasingly unhappy and she finally left him. It was, in her words, 'an untenable time and I didn't want any more of it'.

Pattie and Eric were together for fourteen years, during which time he wrote 'Wonderful Tonight' about her.

Pattie: 'I was maybe pretty, but beautiful is something else.'

George Harrison: 'I remember thinking I just want more. This isn't it. Fame is not the goal. Money is not the goal. To be able to know how to get peace of mind, how to be happy, is something you don't just stumble across. You've got to search for it.'

Another Boyd sister, Jenny, was the inspiration for Donovan's 'Jennifer Juniper', he had a crush on her but they were never an 'item'. She went on to marry Mick Fleetwood and later, Ian Wallace of King Crimson.

'When you love
a woman, it's the God
in her that you see'

George Harrison

Heloísa Pinheiro

'The Girl from Ipanema' 1962

This song was initially created for a musical comedy that Vinicius de Moraes was working on with his collaborator, Antonio Carlos Jobim.

It was during a recording session of the track in New York with Joao Gilberto, Antonio Jobim and Stan Getz, that they decided they needed an English version of the song, and lyricist Norman Gimbel came on board. Astrud Gilberto, Joao's wife, was the best English speaker of the assembled gang and was consequently picked to sing the English verses. Untrained and natural, Astrud captured something fragile and special.

GIMBEL: 'It's the oldest story in the world, the beautiful girl goes by, and men pop out of manholes and fall out of trees and are whistling and going nuts, and she just keeps going by. That's universal.'

Ipanema is a seaside area in southern Rio de Janeiro, there was a cafe/bar that the young Heloísa Enieda Menezes Paes Pinto would pass or call into (to buy cigarettes for her mum) on a regular basis, 'tall and tan and young and lovely' she would generally exit the scene to wolf whistles from the male punters.

Pre-dating the Beatles, this song was an easy-listening masterpiece that introduced a worldwide audience to the Brazilian bossa nova. It won the 1965 Grammy for Record of the Year.

One of the best covers of this track (in my opinion) is by the mighty Lou Rawls.

Linda McCartney

'Maybe I'm Amazed'
Paul McCartney 1969

Written after the Beatles split, Paul pays tribute to Linda for being his rock during the complicated disentanglement of his life up to that point.

He has said it's the song he'd like to be remembered for.

Yoko Ono

'Woman' John Lennon 1980

This is an ode to John's wife Yoko Ono.

He said it was him as a grown-up man, revisiting the song he wrote as a Beatle, 'Girl'... Whilst being very much an accolade to Yoko, in John's inimitable universal greater good style, it's meant for all women.

For a sobering look at misconception and fear, have a look at Al Capp visiting John and Yoko's bed-in in Montreal 1969

Janet Rigsbee

'Crazy Love' Van Morrison 1970

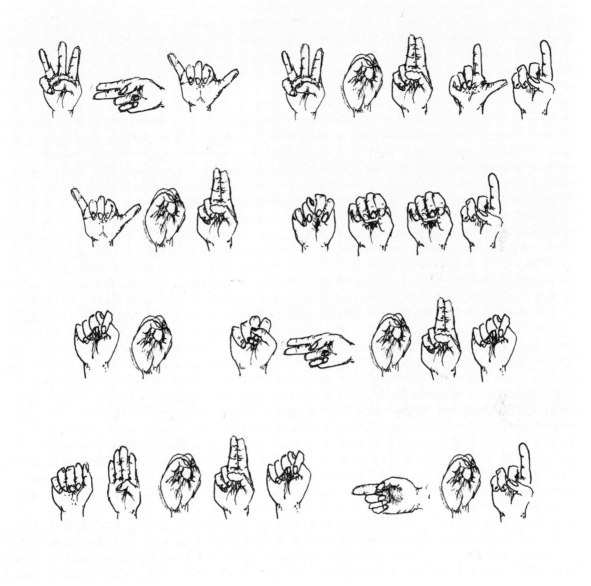

Burmese girls smoking the curious big white cheroots of the country.
Burmese women and girls enjoy much personal freedom
and are fond of gay apparel and social intercourse

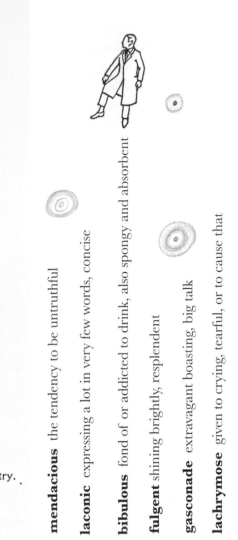

mendacious the tendency to be untruthful

laconic expressing a lot in very few words, concise

bibulous fond of or addicted to drink, also spongy and absorbent

fulgent shining brightly, resplendent

gasconade extravagant boasting, big talk

lachrymose given to crying, tearful, or to cause that

etiolated to become weakened, whitening of a plant by excluding light, drained of colour

DANDELION

mimsy ineffectual, failing to interest, prim

Roast Pigeon. An invalid or convalescent will often enjoy a simply prepared
bird such as a pigeon. It should not be dried in the cooking, and should be
temptingly garnished with watercress

I can only buy a banana if it's on its own. If I can't, I will resort to a banana yoghurt. I can almost hear the bananas crying when people snap one off a bunch.

SARAH – SOUTHAMPTON

I texted my husband the other day to ask 'fancy lunch'. Predictive text sent 'panty lunch'. I'm sure you can guess his reply.

KELLY

Our front door swells in the damp weather. When someone buzzes on the intercom I often have to yell PUSH PUSH PUSH! like a midwife.

MARY – BRIGHTON

The lightswitch in my living room broke about nine months ago. Rather than fixing it, I bought a candelabra and live my evenings by candlelight.

PETE – DERBY

My big sister officially changed her name when she was sixteen (Phyllis to Philippa). When my little brother Ian and I realized this was possible we went to the village post office to change ours. Me to Barry (after Sheen I think) and Ian to Toucan. The postmistress phoned Mum and Dad and we were marched home.

FERGUS

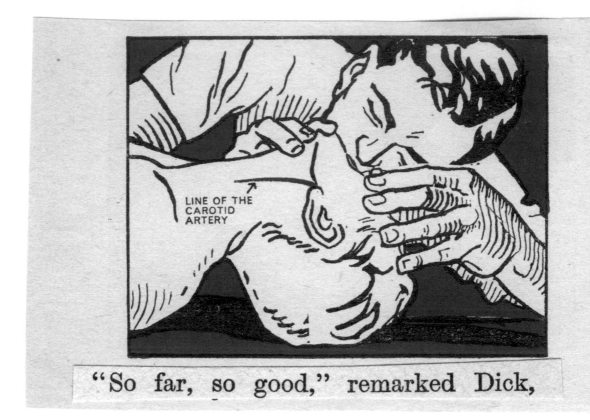

"So far, so good," remarked Dick,

It's an age old conversation starter –
if you could travel back in time,
where would you go?
There are several things to consider here.
How long am I going for?
Am I allowed to take anything with me?
Will I arrive 'wherever' naked?
Now I don't want to be a killjoy, but I
remember a time before duvets were the
norm, so I'm already apprehensive.
Regarding women's rights I'd imagine I
could be coshed quite quickly, and
bearing in mind the lack of female toilets
now, basic needs are going to be tricky.
Wherever you went, it would be awful.

Who, from your past would you say thank you to if you could?

Just hatched—but looking remarkably like a human centenarian.

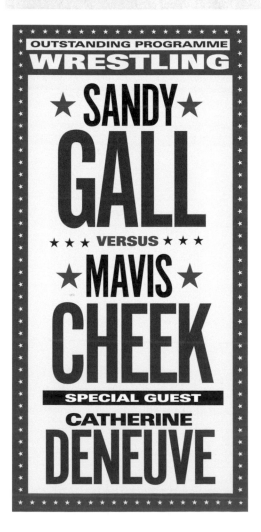

OUTSTANDING PROGRAMME
WRESTLING

★ SANDY ★
GALL

★★★ VERSUS ★★★

★ MAVIS ★
CHEEK

SPECIAL GUEST
CATHERINE
DENEUVE

Guess whose facial hair
MISCELLANY

① ② ③

④ ⑤ ⑥

⑦ ⑧ ⑨

⑩ ⑪ ⑫

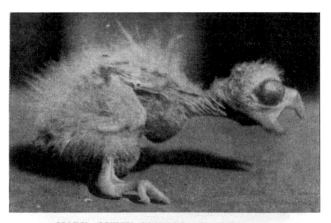

MARY, QUEEN CONSORT OF GEORGE V
Equally with King George V, Queen Mary shared in the love
and loyalty of the British peoples, and her regal appearance
never failed to arouse admiration. She endeared herself to
all by her many charitable acts and unfailing sense of duty.

Years ago my wife and I returned to a car park after walking the dog. We put Cuddy back into the car, and because it was autumn we spent ten minutes running around trying to catch leaves for good luck, screaming and shouting. We stopped when we realized that the car next to ours had two occupants, watching us whilst eating sandwiches.

BEN AND CHARLOTTE

My sister's cat wore a collar with a magnet on it to operate the cat flap. He once came home with a fork and teaspoon stuck to his collar, and a very strange look on his face.

ANDREA – GRANTHAM

When I draw the curtains at night, I move things off the windowsill so they don't feel left out.

ROMILLY – PRUDHOE

I had a dream about running up behind Bruce Willis at a party and tickling him. He was livid.

SARAH – CHESHIRE

One year, my mother dressed me as an OXO cube. This consisted of seven-year-old me inside two large cardboard boxes wrapped in tin foil, with two holes for legs, two for arms and one for my head. She then sent me to a roller disco.

CLAIRE

Translate cockney legend TUBBY ISAAC'S sentences and find the answers in the grid...

K	C	U	T	N	R	T	L	O	P	T	E	C	A	R	T	A	O	B	R
H	E	P	A	R	T	D	N	A	Y	N	O	P	J	L	F	N	Y	U	V
Y	R	U	W	B	O	Z	U	C	K	I	Z	P	V	R	S	F	B	T	E
B	I	G	O	T	H	U	Q	U	W	H	O	R	O	G	W	A	O	C	T
E	S	E	X	T	O	N	B	L	A	K	E	G	E	S	D	T	E	H	A
R	W	O	C	D	N	A	L	L	U	B	A	B	C	U	W	C	V	E	L
P	C	X	R	P	O	J	L	S	E	N	D	Y	B	O	X	U	E	R	P
A	L	F	O	N	E	A	P	T	D	A	N	N	A	O	J	H	D	S	A
S	O	W	S	B	I	M	S	T	Q	I	N	N	J	M	I	G	N	H	N
S	O	I	Y	D	V	J	O	C	U	P	D	D	O	W	M	F	A	O	I
A	P	P	L	E	S	A	N	D	P	E	A	R	S	X	M	L	M	O	H
K	T	O	E	Y	D	R	S	L	I	R	I	U	Q	T	Y	D	A	K	C
N	H	J	E	G	R	E	S	G	R	U	N	B	L	A	R	R	D	E	M
I	E	U	W	C	J	A	H	M	T	H	E	Y	C	K	I	I	A	Z	D
D	L	N	H	B	F	T	G	T	D	C	R	M	V	J	D	B	F	O	F
N	O	U	S	D	I	L	N	I	B	T	S	U	D	Y	D	Y	N	E	A
A	O	K	V	R	W	G	L	T	O	P	I	R	W	F	L	K	U	V	E
N	P	G	F	I	S	E	C	M	F	X	O	R	U	M	E	C	O	I	L
E	H	J	T	A	E	M	F	O	S	E	T	A	L	P	N	I	D	R	A
P	I	S	W	Y	X	H	S	T	O	O	R	Y	S	I	A	O	W	C	E
B	A	D	T	R	E	B	R	E	H	S	L	Z	G	L	C	P	I	R	T

I'll hail us a CAB
Ooo a lovely bowl of SOUP
It's up the STAIRS
Let me get my BOOTS on
I could murder a CURRY
Let's round up the KIDS
Will you join me for a FAG
I'll have to ask the WIFE
Well that's a load of CRAP
I'm going up the ROAD
Let's have a LOOK
I'm having a nice STEAK for my dinner
He's kicked up a right STINK
It's all over my FACE
I'll kick him up the ARSE
I'm just nipping out for a WIDDLE
Give us a tune on the PIANO
A lovely cup of TEA
We've had a right ROW last night...
I don't BELIEVE it
I'm going down the PUB
Just give me FEET a rub
Could you give the CAR a wash
It turns out he's a THIEF
I'm dying for a SHIT
She's been in a terrible STATE
Listen, I won't say a WORD
He's my BEST MATE

IMPERFECT FEATURES

Shortening of the Nose

Before Treatment

After Treatment

A BADLY SHAPED NOSE, OUTSTANDING EARS, RED VEINS, LINES ROUND THE EYES, MOLES, or a face which is prematurely aged can so easily destroy your self-confidence. Write for an appointment for a free Consultation with one who has 25 years' experience in correcting these defects, to Box 121, "Health & Efficiency," c/o Spiers Service Ltd., 69 Fleet Street, London, E.C.4.

THREE ROYAL BROTHERS

Box 316.

OWNER of small well found and comfortable MOTOR CRUISER (centrally heated) invites enquiries from single men who would care for short coastal cruises or week-ends board, and are fit, willing to lend a hand in running ship, keen on the sea and naturism. No sailing experience necessary. Write Box 314.

POSING GOODS!!!

Obtainable only from :
E. A. STANLEY
the Actual Maker (All Post Free)
SILK POSING POUCH 1/-, best 2/-,
SILK POSING SLIP 1/6. FIG LEAF 2/-, with no waistband. ART SILK SLIP elastic waist and legs 2/-, best 2/9. POSING CLOTH 2/9. Imtn. LEOPARD POUCH 2/9. LIGHTWEIGHT JOCK STRAP 2/9. DE LUXE 3/6. COMFY SUSPENSORY SILK 2/9. Mention size and colour required when ordering. ILLUSTRATED LISTS FREE, stamp for sealed envelope.
Goods sent plain wrapper.
631, Forest Rd., London, E.17. 'Phone Lar. 1915

THROWING THE JAVELIN

Ten comedians' catchphrases you might include in any conversation that would be grasped immediately...

Stylish Snippets

Never, ever tumble dry your bra

Remove the 'vintage' scent of clothing by spritzing pieces with a mixture of vodka diluted with water (though avoid using this on silks and satins)

V-necks give an illusion of a looooonger torso

Children, drunks and leggings NEVER lie

Put smelly shoes into a bag and then into the freezer to deodorize

Every wardrobe needs a black turtleneck

The perfect pencil skirt should hover over your knee

Window cleaner spray restores patent leather shoes, bags, belts etc., easily

Wear your new leather jacket in the rain to break it in

I've were so expensive in the middle ages that women were specifically given money to buy them.

MUSICAL MASHUP
THE LION KING AND I

Colorado house-wife Virginia Tighe said that she had been a 19th-century Irishwoman in a previous life.

Things I own that look like Jennifer Saunders

ROBERT DOUGALL

Here's our boy Monty 'The Monts', Mouse Master General.

LUCINDA

Our elderly tom cat Jarvis clambered into a bowl of crisps for a pee in front of several startled guests. Once finished he clambered out as if nothing had happened and walked away.

PAUL – WIMBORNE

Our ginger tom is called Vlad (after the impaler). He attacks passers-by in our street. It wouldn't be so bad if we didn't live in a cul-de-sac with a school. I had to get a warning printed in their weekly newsletter asking kids not to pet him after three attacks in twenty-four hours.

JULES – COLCHESTER

YOU WILL NEED: ● A large chocolate roll ● A packet of 6 mini choc rolls ● One fat croissant ● One chocolate finger ● Chocolate Buttons (with white ones and in various sizes) ● Jelly snake (or similar) for the collar ● Toothpicks

Dachs in a dash

*The wonderful **Bary Merry** shows you how to make this delightful, no-cook, easy-make, doggy cake*

Take 3 mini rolls and cut 2 in half for the legs. Cut the last one about an inch or so thick, this will be the neck.

Place the 4 halves into leg positions and add toothpicks into the middles.

Place the larger chocolate roll on top.

Decide where the head end is and add the little neck piece with a toothpick. Add the chocolate finger to the rear end.

Slice one side of the croissant to make the dog's second ear...

... and secure with a toothpick.

Carefully attach the head to the neck piece.

Melt a little chocolate over a mug of hot water and use this to glue on the eyes and the nose.

Add the finishing touches... the proper eyes and a jelly snake for the collar... this will need securing with a toothpick.

WARNING: this cake is a choking hazard

tea · roses · dogs · singing · clean sheets · freesias · bees · york stone · dawn · ginger cats · toddlers shoes · lipstick · dappled light · lemony yellow · twilight · sparrows · streams · robins · wrens · smell of toast · laughing · jam · individual style · moss · sunshine · eau de cologne · every single member of my family · having nice nails · feathers · woodlands · birch trees · hospitality · pearls · drawing · driving · a big view · dunes · marble · a good brush · pottery · bubbles · generosity · butterflies · moral fibre · puppies · eggs · silver · clear quartz · grown ups · children · music · swing · jigsaws · making salads · coffee · oaks · coming home · craftsmen · the noises of water · sailing · cool breezes · clean washing · passion · talking · kindness · progress · artistic endeavour · eyes · stone circles · font · theatre · May · mosaic · reading · ants · succulents · thoughtfulness · pops of colour · jugs · beaches · puffins · my glorious friends · my garden · good company · solutions · wit · beech trees · nuts · fire · sheep · donkeys · rock pooling · flasks · comfy shoes · vodka & tonic · a great script · old souls · fractals · honey · sparkly things · pennies dropping · mist · falling in love · great audiences · making things · beads · clean teeth · fresh flowers · subtlety · velvet · a great coat · a big sky · road trips · carving · dew · space · goldfinches · candlelight · roast chicken · cheese · harmony · walking · honesty · blackbirds · wilderness · intelligence · manners · creatives · my god children · apples · worn shoes · gems · cooking · confidence · paint · rude health · ingenuity · ART

Can you fill up this page with things YOU LOVE

Phenomenal Woman

Pretty women wonder where my secret lies.
I'm not cute or built to suit a fashion model's size
But when I start to tell them,
They think I'm telling lies.
I say,
It's in the reach of my arms,
The span of my hips,
The stride of my step,
The curl of my lips.
I'm a woman
Phenomenally.
Phenomenal woman,
That's me.

I walk into a room
Just as cool as you please,
And to a man,
The fellows stand or
Fall down on their knees.
Then they swarm around me,
A hive of honey bees.
I say,
It's the fire in my eyes,
And the flash of my teeth,
The swing in my waist,
And the joy in my feet.
I'm a woman
Phenomenally.

Phenomenal woman,
That's me.

Men themselves have wondered
What they see in me.
They try so much
But they can't touch
My inner mystery.
When I try to show them,
They say they still can't see.
I say,
It's in the arch of my back,
The sun of my smile,
The ride of my breasts,
The grace of my style.
I'm a woman
Phenomenally.
Phenomenal woman,
That's me.

Now you understand
Just why my head's not bowed.
I don't shout or jump about
Or have to talk real loud.
When you see me passing,
It ought to make you proud.
I say,
It's in the click of my heels,
The bend of my hair,
the palm of my hand,
The need for my care.
'Cause I'm a woman
Phenomenally.
Phenomenal woman,
That's me.

BY MAYA ANGELOU

"LET ME SHOW YOU
THE MAN YOU CAN BECOME"

Says George Walsh, the World's Greatest Body-Builder and Official Olympic Games Coach

Pupil R.S., age 20. A product of 'Body-Bulk' Training.

"Simply state your age and measurements (height, chest, upper arm, wrist, hips, thigh and ankle). In return I will send you a detailed statement of your personal possibilities—tell you the exact body weight and measurements which you can reach by scientific 'Body-Bulk' training. You will also receive a copy of my booklet 'George Walsh Presents Body-Bulk.'"

No apparatus is required

This Service is ABSOLUTELY FREE

THE FAMOUS
"BODY-BULK"

course of home training, compiled and conducted by George Walsh, the world's greatest body-building authority, has already raised thousands of weaklings to super strength and physique. Whether you are thin and under weight, an ordinary well-developed man or a strength athlete who wants to move into a higher body-weight division—the "Body-Bulk" course is **GUARANTEED** to lift you to the highest degree of solid, powerful muscular development.

● COMPLETE COURSE 30/-

Send P.O. or Cash, with age, body-weight, measurements, and increases desired. Or send measurement details for a Free Analysis of your possibilities.

A TYPICAL "BODY-BULK" RESULT
Name—J.L.W., Wakefield.

	At Commencement	End of 1st Lesson	End of 2nd Lesson	End of 3rd Lesson
Height ...	5ft. 9½in.	5ft. 9¾in.	5ft. 10in.	5ft. 10½in.
Weight ...	10-9	11-4	11-13	12-5
Biceps ...	12½in.	13¼in.	14in.	14¼in.
Neck ...	15½in.	16in.	16½in.	16¾in.
Thighs ...	20½in.	21½in.	22½in.	23in.

These lessons can be carried out in the smallest space. The course lasts from 3 to 6 months according to the increases desired. Time required—15 to 25 minutes daily.

WALSH INSTITUTE of PHYSICAL TRAINING

DEPT. HE., 29 SOUTHAMPTON BUILDINGS, CHANCERY LANE, LONDON, W.C.I.

A FLAG, HALF-MAST.

Lon Chaney as Phantom of the Opera (1925)

THE WIND.

Catherine Cookson book (title unknown) about a jilted woman who works in a dress shop and tells rival: "I don't serve whores". Will pay costs. ~~Xxxxxxxx~~horn ~~Xxxxxxx~~well, Leeds, Yorks ~~xxxxxx~~

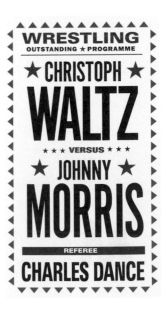

WRESTLING
OUTSTANDING ★ PROGRAMME
★ CHRISTOPH ★
WALTZ
★ ★ ★ VERSUS ★ ★ ★
★ JOHNNY ★
MORRIS
REFEREE
CHARLES DANCE

When my sister started suffering menopausal symptoms she purchased a special two-piece magnet that you placed either side of the front of your pants next to your belly button. But while she was at work one day she opened the metal filing cabinet and got stuck to it! She was freed by a hysterical colleague and never lived it down.

KIRSTEEN – SHROPSHIRE

I glued the hem of my nightie to my forehead on Christmas morning knowing that sixteen people were coming to lunch!

ANON

I have a friend who lives in a village in Dorset who invited me up one evening. He texted to ask if I would bring a takeaway of my choice on the way. I texted 'I've already eaten but I'll pick you one up'. 'Pick' came out as 'sick'!

My cat Henry's hobby appears to be opening all the cupboard doors in the house. Not a day goes by when I'm not drawn upstairs by the unmistakeable sound of the cat opening the wardrobe doors.

SARAH – CHESHIRE

My husband can only say 'coffee' as though he's a waitress in a New York diner – pronouncing it 'cworfee'.

CAROLINE – OVERTON

BILLY WILDER

I wish I'd met him. I bet he was great company

Good Morning Judge 10cc
creative in a myriad of ways ♡ ♡ Underated GENIUS of 10cc still irks me, like XTC....
Fabulous opener. proper cleansing from the show before...

Say it Ain't So, Joe Dakota Staton wonderful voice, effortless, quirky high leaps
..nice production..brassy... amuse me...

Hit the Road Jack Shirley Horn keeping with the girls, strong version, clearly
accompanying herself on piano, timing is perfect, not convinced by the
rest of the band tho'

Killer Queen Queen piano again to scan from last song....
Their first US hit. another meticulous & gripping song. crowd pleaser... wonderful details

It Won't Be Long Clarence 'Frogman' Henry rhythm & blues, easy style, mixes things
up for my purposes, I find him appealing
cos it's simple, no frills really...

1980 Could You Be Loved Bob Marley ♡ ♡ ♡
Classic, nuff said, is 'Babylon by Bus' my fave album? hmmmm......

1992 You Look Like Rain Morphine This is so sexy it's an eyebrow raiser. The talents
of Mark Sandman, messing with our minds. from the album Good

1970 And It Stoned Me Van Morrison ♡ ♡ ...I like a link just for me, morphine & stoned & all that....
Classic. I ♡ van ♡ I'm obsessed with water & it's mysticism, Van got stoned
from a stream & never forgot it.

Cracking Up Nick Lowe another creative giant, lovely trawling through his catalogue.

1961 Runaway Del Shannon a favourite from my youth, mum & dad still jive to this
if we insist !!

'55' Down Bound Train Chuck Berry Wonderful, unusual track, about booze...
driving rhythm, Genius of Chuck
odd fade in & out ...one of the first

1982 Night Nurse Gregory Isaacs times it was used
Greg Greee's biggest hit... classy yet filthy apparently.

Fairchild Willie West taking the previous beat & mixing it up
I've put it in as an answer to G.Isaacs really but I ♡ this song a lot well worth
listening to is willy.

1982 The Bitterest Pill The Jam
a real mood changer on this list, but a great song to (possibly) end on...

La Vie en Rose Bert Kaempfert instrumental for under a min snippet
lovely version, heavy with perfume if we're pushed for time.

Love Me Forever The Skatalites
Just to wind up the roots rockin element with a bit of joy, lovely & easy

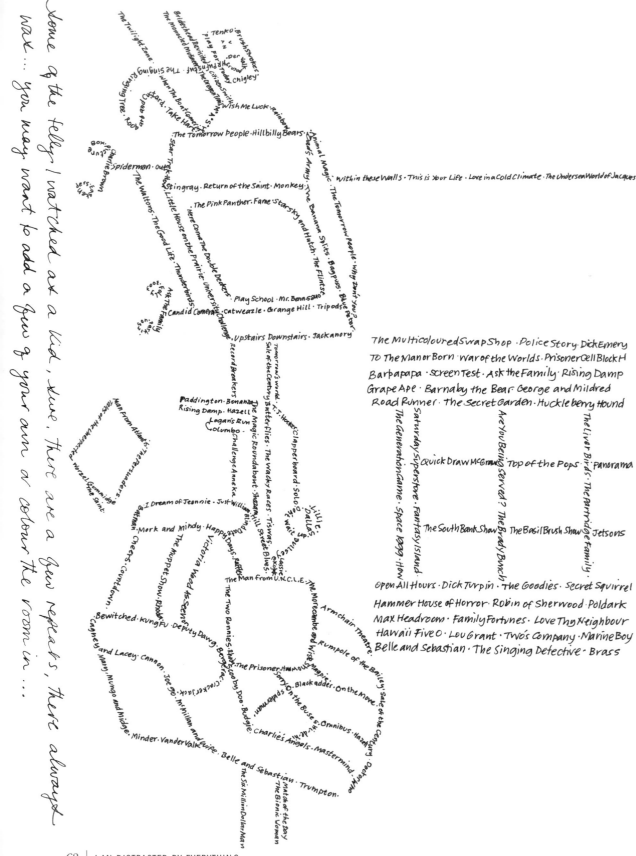

SOUNDS GOOD 1

Read the story and fill in the blanks from the choices below.

Twenty-four-year-old Val Taylor stared at the Beatnik blond boy and was convinced he was flirting.
In the background _____ sang _____on a mix tape. Was it a sign?
He twinkled his green eyes and offered her another chocolate malted milk biscuit. 'You said you like
to write poetry?'
Val decided to match his flirt, and lowered her green eyes to the floor. 'I don't really like to share it
with anyone.'
He lifted her face, 'John Lennon once said that you should 'never deny your mind's flight.' Then
he kissed her. Beautifully. Val was surprised at the quality of the kiss. In one astonishing moment,
everything she thought she knew turned over. He stopped kissing her, jumped up and left. Val stood in
the middle of the room and decided that's what you get when you snog someone five years younger.
As _____started to sing _____ on the mix tape, he came back in to the room. 'There is
something I need to say and if I don't say it now, I'll never know. I've watched you for ages, Val.
I really like you. I think you are the sexiest, funniest, most phenomenal woman I have ever met, and I
know I'm not your 'type' and I might be punching above my weight but I would really like to
romance you.'
Val stared at the flustered nineteen-year-old standing by the door. The words that had just fallen out of
his mouth had taken her breath away. He looked at her with an adoration she'd never known before.
She slowly walked over, took his face in her hands and smiled at him
His heartbeat was in his mouth.
'Can I ask you something?'
'Yes, Val?'
'Can I have another biscuit?' From that moment of laughter on, they were inseparable.
They moved in with each other three weeks later and were married within the year. Mr and Mrs Adams
graduated from college and moved from their beloved party flat to a house in the middle of the town.
They lay in bed listening to the radio and revelled in their new home.
'What are we going to do with all this space, Mr Adams?'
'Fill it with our stuff, our love and our memories, my beautiful wife.'
As he held her in his arms, _____ sang _____ . It was definitely a sign...

Music Choices

The Shamen – Ebeneezer Goode

Otis Redding – Try A Little Tenderness

The Beatles – I Am the Walrus

Meatloaf – Bat Out of Hell

Bob Dylan – I Want You

The Prodigy – Smack My Bitch Up

Crosb, Stills & Nash – Our House

Queen – Fat Bottomed Girls

TELLY SAVALAS

DRESS UP
Miriam

castanets

viking horn

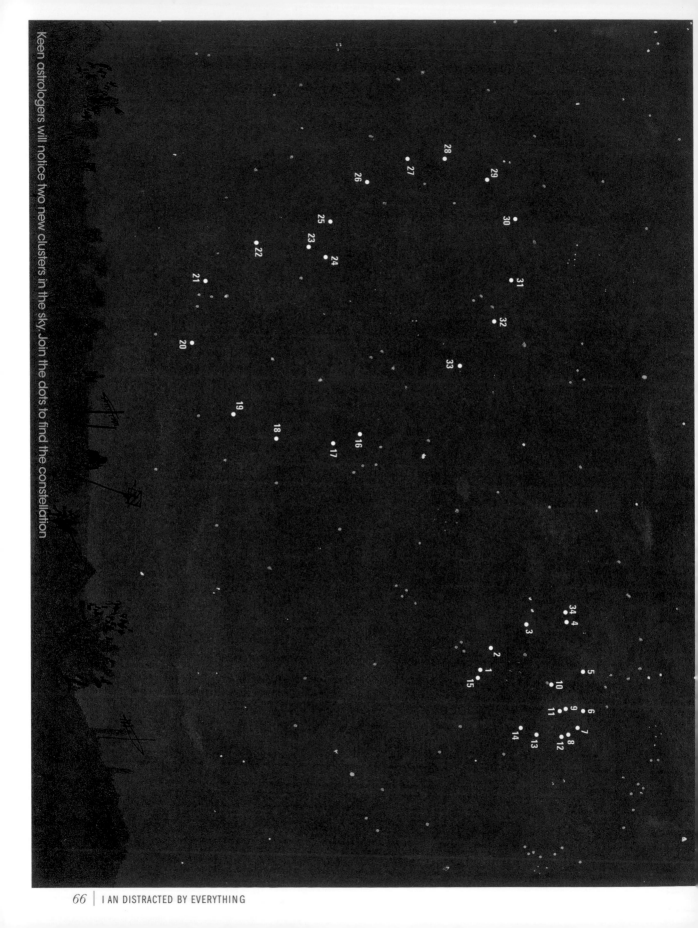

Keen astrologers will notice two new clusters in the sky. Join the dots to find the constellation

My black Great Dane ate her dog trainer's car keys in her second class. Since then she has eaten all sorts, but by far the worst is tennis balls. She swallows them whole and they come out the other end whole. The expression on her face is hilarious!

EMILY – KENT

I once asked a poorly friend, by text, 'Are you coping?' She received 'Are you boring?'

WILL – BRIXTON

I've spent the afternoon tiling an alcove in the kitchen, while my husband went to a football match. I haven't told him what I've been up to. I'm going to wait and see how long it'll take him to notice.

LINDA – KENT

I have to cook the lasagne while my wife watches me. She sits on her bar stool, drinking piña coladas and colouring in her mindfulness cat book.

GARRY – BRISTOL

My lurcher called Merlin pulled the freezer away from the wall, chewed the cable, opened the freezer and unwrapped a sea trout. When I came home he was in his basket licking the ultimate fish ice lolly. Imagine the smell.

DAVID ON THE WIRRAL

Do trees talk to each other?

Of course they do, but **how** they do it is fabulous.

Imagine a tree is a body and you'd imagine the canopy and all we can see is the important part, but actually if a tree was your body, it'd be like your head and arms buried up to your torso – the canopy is the equivalent of you from the waist up, legs and sex organs out in the air – the thinking part of a tree is underground.

The seed finds its spot, it germinates and, despite all odds, makes it through to being a sapling, but now it's got to work to keep itself nourished and healthy. It must tether itself to the position it's found itself in and it's going to need help because it can't just up sticks and move, it's very important that it gets on with the neighbours.

A tree's best friend is fungus – any variety of fungi will do because they essentially work in the same way.

The threadlike mycelium are now firmly interwoven between the trees. The fungi cells wrap around the roots of the trees like socks, creating a bridge for any tree to exchange information with its neighbours; so a little birch tree at the edges of the wood, leafless in winter, may find itself low in nitrogen... It send its message out via this fungal internet... And a deciduous fir with a glut of nitrogen is able to pass on the nutrient to keep the birch healthy.

The mycelium are constantly reaching out, probing entire areas looking for nutrients, breaking down organic matter and degrading poisons, not only talking to their chums, but providing the equivalent of a road system to exchange and receive goods.

Fungus is clever enough to speak every tree's language – the ultimate translator. It understands the stresses of every species, passing on information from one to another, from nutritional needs, to warning the trees that a swarm of leaf-eating insects are on their way... You might want to up the ante on your toxins, lads.

They're even sensitive to footfall – the mycelium, extending out beyond the edges of the woods, know you're coming.

The Dancing Tree (codariocalyx motorius)

Trees and plants are sensitive to sound. Various experiments were started in the 1960s, and different music played to plants was found to strengthen them (classical and jazz), or weaken them (heavy rock)... Science pooh poohed this as hippy nonsense, but the practice remains buoyant and some people swear by it.

The Dancing Tree is very obviously susceptible to music and song, moving itself quickly enough for the eye to see. These plants can be trained to react more quickly, rather like training a sportsperson to strengthen muscles and improve various strategies, and as anyone will tell you, this requires memory. This tree has a memory.

So, there's that big old tree you've admired on your walk... its built itself an entire network of mushrooms and toadstools and reached an awe-inspiring age being really good at not only getting its own needs met, but sharing its surpluses and knowledge to the surrounding members of the woods.

A good mix of different trees keeps a wood healthy. Every tree has a different part to play, contributing to the whole, from housing animals that spread seeds or pollen, to being able to cope with different soils or weather. For these reasons, mixed forests re-heal themselves vey quickly, as they have the multi-layered back-up that a diverse woodland offers. A forest fire or hurricane could decimate a single-species tree plantation because it hasn't got the collection of different mates to augment good judgements and procedures.

Because each tree is rooted to the ground it has to be very particular who it's mixing with, so one type of tree may be more welcome than another so that no one's competing for resources. Trees are complex, they're continually screening information – when to flower or lie dormant, when to grab what they can and flourish, and these are critical decisions, something the tree itself is deciding, co-ordinating its actions to what it's sensing within its environment. It is, therefore, acting with intelligence.

The circuit of communication used by the rooting system of trees and plants – and I mean at a cellular and molecular level – bears strikingly similarities to that of our own human nervous system. The cells may be different but they're very definitely creating circuits of communication akin to a vertebrate's nervous system. Scientists cannot argue with that – and you know what that mob's like.

A 'mother tree', one of those big old astonishing ones we are often drawn to, is capable of passing retained knowledge on to new saplings. Increasing the new growth's resilience will secure its own future and there is some evidence that a tree can recognize its own seed, favouring it (rather like humans), going without to enable sufficient nutrition to get to the sapling, or halting its own root growth to leave room for the new baby one to flourish.

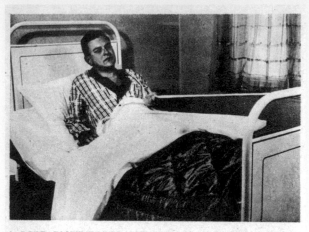

A ROPE FASTENED TO THE END OF THE BED ENABLES
AN INVALID TO PULL HIMSELF UP EASILY

ROMAN NUMERALS with Arabic Equivalents			
I.. 1	XI..11	XXI.. 21	D.. 500
II.. 2	XII..12	XXX.. 30	DC.. 600
III.. 3	XIII..13	XL.. 40	DCC.. 700
IV.. 4	XIV..14	L.. 50	DCCC.. 800
V.. 5	XV..15	LX.. 60	CM.. 900
VI.. 6	XVI..16	LXX.. 70	M..1,000
VII.. 7	XVII..17	LXXX.. 80	MM..2,000
VIII.. 8	XVIII..18	XC.. 90	$\overline{IV}$..4,000
IX.. 9	XIX..19	C..100	$\overline{V}$..5,000
X..10	XX..20	CC..200	$\overline{IX}$..9,000

Amazing Hair-Growth
AFTER BALDNESS—BY USING KOTALKO

Mrs. Cussell, of 30, Hayhill Rd., Ipswich,
writes:—

"Dear Sirs.—When I commenced with the use of Kotalko my head was bare and my scalp quite shiny, except for a very small place where there remained about a handful of hair.

"I had used many preparations, in fact, the trouble was not through neglect, but none of them had prevented the existing condition.

"You can imagine the amazement of myself and friends when, after the use of one box of Kotalko, new hair could be seen all over my head, and after three boxes had been used, my head was covered with a new growth of thick hair, which continued to grow until now I have hair down to my waist in splendid condition."

KOTALKO
TRUE HAIR GROWER

Send threepence in stamps to-day for a Testing Box of Kotalko and particulars of many other remarkable cases of growth after baldness, falling hair stopped, and dandruff eliminated. Kotalko is splendid for children's hair and for all cases of thin and brittle hair or other hirsutal troubles. Address:—

J. H. Brittain Ltd., 2, Percy St. (74 E.K.), London.

48.—BUSH TRIMMING.

One of the advantages associated with the work of trimming the bushes and hedges of front gardens is that he who undertakes it can readily observe where his services are likely to be required. The house-holder who is away from home from early morning till late in the day has no opportunity of attending to this work himself, yet he likes to see the front of the house kept trim and neat. Thus bush-trimming may be the source of continuous employment for the long summer evenings after the ordinary day's work is done.

THROWING THE HAMMER

HAVE YOU DONE ANY OF THE FOLLOWING TODAY?

☐ Disguised criticism behind a compliment

☐ Complained of unfair treatment

☐ Complained of being under appreciated

☐ Deliberately procrastinated

☐ Made mistakes on purpose

☐ Denied having any responsibility

☐ Gossiped negatively

☐ Repeatedly teased someone

☐ Been repeatedly sarcastic

☐ Blamed anyone or anything

☐ Exaggerated your health issues

☐ Shown stubbornness

☐ Been unwilling to engage in constructive chat

☐ Made anyone feel uncomfortable

CONGRATULATIONS
you've been passively aggressive

I ♡ donkeys. so does dad

10 FEMALE CHEFS
GO

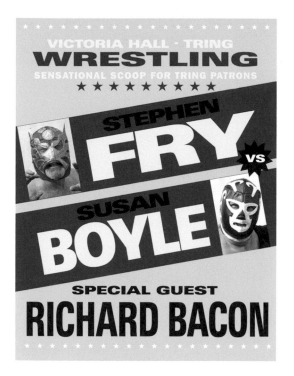

Camp cooking can be practised in the Troop room in winter—but mind where you toss the pancake

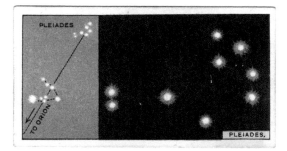

A photographer this week said:

'Could you smile bigger because your teeth are very current.'

I didn't stay long.

I just misheard a bit of commentary on a documentary:

'John shits his focus.'

It made complete sense.

There are all kinds of novel parties which might suit a boy or girl just growing out of the parties of childhood. What about a gramophone evening, when guests each bring a favourite record and after a buffet supper sit round the lounge and play their individual choices? This might be lightened by square dancing to the gramophone or the tape recorder, if you are lucky enough to possess one.

1957

... and then Chuck Berry turned up and the whole bloody lot went off.

Murder Mystery Puzzle

Play the sleuth in this puzzle and find 13 potentially deadly weapons before someone gets hurt.

"So long, Tommy," he said quietly. "Good hunting."
Then, without a backward glance he strode away through
the jungle in the direction of the river.

My hubby waves to skips. He says they must be lonely just sitting there having rubbish thrown into them.

GILL – STAFFORD

When my sister and I went into a lift when we were younger, she told me you had to face into the corner and stand on one leg, otherwise the lift would drop to the ground and we'd die. I'm not sure what's more worrying: that I believed her, or the fact that my mum, who was with us, never said a word.

TERESA – HARLOW

My daughter ordered bananas with her online shop from Tesco and received a bottle of bleach as a replacement.

ANGELA – NEW MALDEN

I had a senior moment at my son's 5th birthday party. We were playing hide and seek and I decided to hide in the boot of my husband's car. Not long after I had climbed in, I heard the engine start. I assumed it was Neil. I tried calling him but he couldn't hear me. After around fifteen minutes the car stopped, the boot opened, and to my horror I found my neighbour standing staring at me. Slowly, he grabbed the shopping bag next to me and stood back. After I explained what had happened, I told him he was in the wrong car. He then pointed out that I was in his car.

CAROLINE – BRIGHTON

JEAN MUIR

crepe, silk, luxury fabrics, well cut & generally unadorned. The cut would do the whispering while the wearer could stun. An amazing talent. My mate Wendy forced me to buy one & her dresses, if I was to forgive me, in cost a fortune & I wore it to death. Thank you Jean &

started in Liberty's, moved on to Jaeger, by the mid 60's she was running her own label. Grown up elegance, Jersey,

I have lived all my life

in Mountfield, a small village in East Sussex surrounded by ancient woodland. Until comparatively recently, the village was populated mostly by families who had lived there for generations. As small children after WWII, we were all aware that there were certain areas of woodland best avoided towards nightfall and others well known as blessed places where solace could be found in times of trouble.

One wood, known as Castle Wood because of the remains of ancient earthworks, is an area known for atmosphere. I walk it regularly and spend some time on the earthwork meditating, but on one occasion, in early October 1998, something very curious happened.

It was a perfectly still, glorious autumn afternoon. I entered the woodland and immediately felt a heightened awareness. As I approached the main wood up a rutted cart track, the branches of the trees began to move, though I could feel no breeze at all. I slowed my pace, but the wind in the trees became very strong, and as I reached the edge of the earthworks, branches on either side of the path came down and barred my way. Inside the wood, I could see a flock of large black birds, either rooks or crows, flapping around wildly, though they made no cawing noise.

I was brought up to acknowledge and respect the existence of earth spirits and elementals, and, though I was mystified and a little alarmed, I stood my ground and sent a psychic message in greeting to whatever was there, and I appreciated that I was not welcome that day. At the bottom of the track I turned and looked back, and where I had just walked, brambles which had been in the hedgerow had fallen across the path, making it impossible for anyone else to walk in the wood.

On the way home, I called on the village tree warden and told him what had happened. He said that he too had not been 'allowed' into the woods for about three weeks. We were later informed that the Water Board was at that time proposing to make a road right through the wood to a reservoir that supplies Hastings with water. The surveyors encountered such obstacles, difficulties and local opposition that they abandoned the plan and our peaceful, gentle woodland remains untouched but for occasional coppicing.

J L S East Sussex, By email to Fortean Times 2001

Is nature's most perfect packaging the banana or the egg?

I wonder what flies think glass is?

Is Banksy our modern day Zorro?

How much of my life has been spent retrieving balls?

WEATHERCOCK.

The weather-vanes of the majority of our older cathedrals and churches are surmounted by a model of a cock, which is often gilded. In all probability these were originally set up by the old cathedral builders to remind them of the Apostle Peter's denial of Christ, and therefore to serve as a warning.

crepuscular resembling twilight, dim or indistinct

Guess whose facial hair

WRITERS

① ② ③

④ ⑤ ⑥

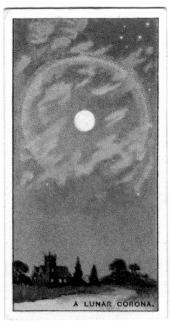

A LUNAR CORONA.

Adeney: in his teens he vowed to become 'the best flute player in the world and to have a huge amount of sex'

& today it's been that when you have a thought, that thought then thinks & either grows with its own volition or dwindles, ready to be found by someone else ... mercurial thoughts blebbing into bigger, fullsome ones

I had a dream about six months ago that Daniel was pestering me to 'go out with him' (ahem) but I resisted and told him I was very happily married. Woke up kicking myself.

CALLY – SUFFOLK

Please can you tell the Daniel Craig snogger he was two timing that night, the rat. He was actually giving me a facial whilst periodically kissing my face sensually.

MELANIE – NORTH YORKSHIRE

I'm making a packet of peppercorn sauce mix before my husband gets back from golf. He loved the one I made last time; little did he know it wasn't due to any culinary skill. I've hidden the packet deep in the bin.

CLAIRE – MACCLESFIELD

Tell Melanie from North Yorks that HER Daniel Craig was clearly an imposter. He was en route with me to the fleshpots of Liverpool City Centre. I ain't lettin' go of this dream.

ANNA – WALLASEY

Concretia. It means the evoking of a memory from the smell of an inanimate object. Who knew?

PETE THE PLUMBER – NOTTINGHAM

the Wed when I got the chance to meet her. Even if she did think Scottish

She succeeded in getting midwives better pay. Yet she was hugely successful as an author of romantic fiction & whilst they're not my cup of tea, she was an independent working mother & I felt

BARBARA CARTLAND

a formidable woman, largely responsible for the introduction of vitamins into the UK. She was a leading advocate of homeopathic medicine. She fought for Gypsy children to

Make a list of items in your home that are at least 50 years old

SOUNDS GOOD 2

Read the story and fill in the blanks from the choices below.

Forty-six-year-old Val Taylor put the key in the lock, opened the door and felt the warmth of the central heating on her face. Doing her best to keep quiet, she crept in to the bedroom, got undressed, climbed in to bed and snuggled up to her husband's familiar furriness.

Sunday morning and _____ was singing _____ on the radio. She smiled as the song took her back to student days of cheap wine and late nights. She sat up as he brought two cups of coffee in to the bedroom. 'Thanks, love. This takes us back, eh?'

He nodded and took a deep breath. 'I want a divorce. All I want are my records and my books. This isn't working for me any more.'

Everything went in to slow motion. Val saw the change immediately. The light had gone out in his eyes. If there had been a cliff, she would have thrown herself off it (not that she was dramatic or anything). The song on the radio changed and _____ started to sing _____. They looked at each other and started to laugh. The confused tears streamed down their faces.

She tried to hug him, but he pulled away. 'How about I go away for a couple of weeks? Give us both some space?' She did.

They agreed no contact for two weeks but the yesterdays blended in to the tomorrows and Val, swallowing her tears, called him. 'Hey you.'

'Hey you' he said. 'Val, I've had a think and I am 80% sure.'

Her heart skipped a beat.

She drove down the motorway with a sense of empowerment, giddy as _____sang _____ on the radio. As soon as she got home, she unpacked, cooked a curry and waited. Hearing the front door she checked herself in the mirror.

'What are you doing here? I thought you were staying away for a bit longer?' he said.

Val stood up and looked at her husband. 'If you're 80% sure, I think twenty-three years is worth fighting for.'

He looked at his wife. 'The other way round.'

'What?' said Val

'I'm 80% sure I want us to finish.'

Val fell to the floor, head in hands, crushed. _____ started to sing _____ on an old mix tape and he turned the music off.

Music Choices

Harry Nilsson – Without You

Joni Mitchel – All I Want

David Bowie – The Laughing Gnome

John Paul Young – Love Is In the Air

Carly Simon – Let the River Run

Marvin Gaye – Let's Get It On

Survivor – The Eye of the Tiger

Matt Monroe – On Days Like These

Madness – Embarrassment

The Faces – Stay With Me

Play on words

The following pictures and numbers represent the titles of well-known plays. Give yourself a bonus for each one you've seen

– – – – –

– – – – – – – – –

– – – – – – – – – – – –

– – – – – – – – – – – – – –

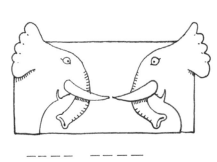

– – – – – – – – – – –

– – – – – – – – – –

– – – – – – – – – – – – – – –
– – – – – – – –

– – – – – –

JULY						
	1	2	3	4	5	☺
7	☺	9	☺	☺	12	☺
14	15	16	☺	18	☺	20
21	22	☺	24	25	26	27
28	29	30	☺			

– – – – – – – – –

– – – – – – – – – – – – – – – – – – –

WHAT'S SO GREAT ABOUT
STINGING
NETTLES?

Fresh nettles traditionally start to appear in March. Winter is naturally a time of self-reflection, planning, and is generally more 'indoors', and with Spring comes growth, movement and promise; but to help us come out of the dormant season we need a 'bridge', and nettles offer some very potent assistance. A masterful neurotive, they can actually order our thoughts to encourage action.

● Essentially, nettles build **healthy blood**. They nourish and cleanse it and as their goodness passes round the body's transport system of veins and arteries, they of course pass through our vital organs, dropping off their goodies as they go.

● They offer a tremendous boost for **kidney function**. Kidneys represent the 'will' in Chinese medicine (which is the capacity to act in a decisive way on any of our desires), so this organ needs to be in tiptop shape to get us moving towards our goals.

● They cleanse the **liver**. Everything we take in to our bodies has to pass through the liver before it can be excreted. This organ is essentially like a weir, so if we can pick up last season's litter and unblock the area it'll work more productively.

● Nettles cleanse the **spleen** (which recycles old red blood cells) and the gall bladder (which aids digestion of fats), and they're also great for the lungs and act like an expectorant.

● The white hairs on the stem of the plant and the underside of the leaves contain formic acid, which is why they 'sting'; some ants have this too. **Formic acid** can be used as a preservative and has antibacterial properties so it's often used in silage to keep the animal feed fresh. The sting can increase **blood circulation** and this can be beneficial around **arthritic joints.**

● **White dead nettles.** They can be found in similar spots as stinging nettles and look very alike, but as the name suggests, they don't sting. They too can be eaten and are very popular with bees.

● Nettles prefer wetter ground and like a high presence of nitrogen like compost heaps or piles of manure.

● Nettles are also **anti-asthmatic**. They reduce haemorrhoids and water retention, they cleanse the digestive system and they support the adrenal glands, which in turn produce our vital hormones, necessary for just about everything to function well, from **blood pressure** to **metabolism**. Great for **anaemia, gout, arthritis** and **eczema**, they work wonders on the **lymphatic system** (which removes waste throughout the body and presides over our immune system). They're also good for **lactation** in nursing mothers, promoting breast milk production, and they've been found to be good for diabetes.

● In men's health, the addition of nettles to the diet peps up the whole gent's veg area, they're great for **testosterone** and inhibit the **prostate**.

● They contain **vitamins A,B,C** and **D**, iron, calcium, manganese, zinc and magnesium, they're good for **urinary disorders**, balancing for **menopause** symptoms, and are a natural **antihistamine**.

● Nettles are best in spring. Pick the top leaves to enable the plant to recover, and once it's got flowers on it leave it alone. (It's not poisonous at this point in its lifecycle, merely 'woody' and not at its best to eat).
● Cooking or drying the plant neutralizes the sting.
● It's a protein-rich vegetable, boosts energy and uplifts you.
● The fresh leaves are great in a soup or a stir-fry.

●It's readily available as tea (which is my preferred way of getting its benefits) but don't overdo it... one mug a day is enough or you'll start to get headaches.

● Don't start me on cordage, it's another brilliant aspect of this helpful plant.

John Nettles: Don't pick him, he'll go potty.

What's on this cats mind?

cavil to raise irritating and trivial objections, find fault with unnecessarily

CIVIC HALL – SOLIHULL

WRESTLING
FOR THE WORLD CHAMPIONSHIP

BOBBY
MOORE
versus
ANTON
LESSER
SPECIAL GUEST
GLENN CLOSE

Stylish Snippets

To stop squeaky shoes put Vaseline under the insoles.

A structured hat should sit ⅛" to ½" above your ears.

Don't ever stuff your wardrobe. Natural fabrics like denim and silk need to breathe 'and relax'

To break-in new shoes, wear socks then blast them with a hot hair dryer

Shaving cream removes stubborn stains on clothes

Of course red and green can be seen!

Static problems? Spray hairspray up your skirt or wipe thighs with tumble dryer sheets

Only wear one grunge item in one outfit (this includes bags)

REMOVING SEA-WATER STAINS FROM BROWN SHOES

SODA

Scrofulus – morally degraded

My twelve-stone Great Dane, Hugo, loves to run down the garden towards the house at full speed and as he comes through the back door, lock his legs up and 'surf' the doormat in to the kitchen. We dare not get in the way as he would flatten us. He loves doing it and always has a sparkle in his eyes afterwards.

DAVID – VAUXHALL

Whenever I hear mention of the World Health Organisation I have to say 'Who?' At first I thought it was funny, now I do it automatically and it's driving me nuts!

STEVE – FARNHAM

I dreamt last night that I saved Rod Stewart's life as his pacemaker was acting up. Once sorted he wrote me a cheque for £148!

CAROL-ANN – CARLISLE

When I was younger I wanted a nice shaggy perm – which were in fashion at the time. My cousin did it for me and I couldn't see how she was getting on as she didn't have a mirror. When she was finished I had what looked like the shampoo and set my mum had. I had to go into school for the last day of term. Sat in the classroom and no one recognized me! I cried for three weeks.

ALISON – ASHFORD

My wake-up moment that I recall aged about ten years was that babies were not born with clothes on.

MOJO

PAUL NEWMAN

PhhhhWwoaarrr

my GO TO Crush after I watched
"THE HUSTLER"

10 Native American Tribes GO

Petroglyphs ↗ ⊙ ⊙ ⊙ ⊙ · ⊙ ⊙ ·

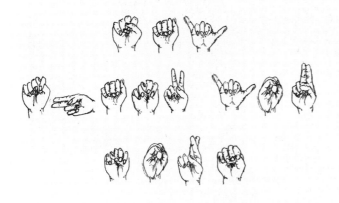

Ten Tube stations beginning with the letter E *GO*

The young recruit reports for duty, checked in by a petty officer.

What you *need* is a rock solid prenup. Ask Paul McCartney.

Pan frying lamb cutlets is an idiot's game

TOWN HALL - BOGNOR REGIS
WRESTLING
WC FIELDS
VS
ELTON JOHN
COMMENTATOR
LULU

I can guarantee that I will never swim in a quarry at night, or go potholing, or be cast in the remake of Tenko.

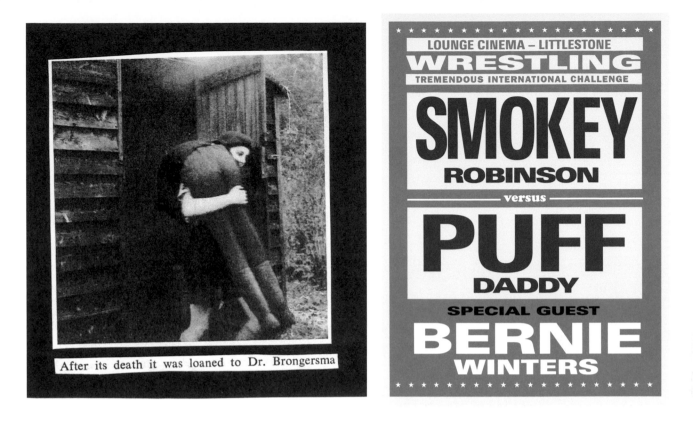

After its death it was loaned to Dr. Brongersma

LOUNGE CINEMA – LITTLESTONE
WRESTLING
TREMENDOUS INTERNATIONAL CHALLENGE
SMOKEY ROBINSON
versus
PUFF DADDY
SPECIAL GUEST
BERNIE WINTERS

It's half ten, I've done my job, it's been a long day and I just want to get home. Company booked me a driver home, an exec cab.

Chatty fella. That's OK.

Ten minutes in he's telling me about his woes, divorce, plans, what he's about … gets on to his sex life and what he likes or not … tells me how he'd pick up women at this health club, you have to have a certain solvency to be a member, so picking up women was easy, women like you to have money, you're a relatively safe bet if you're a member there. Rich pickings. He doesn't draw breath, he's just talking at me.

Goes on to let me know something he has never told a woman before, never told anyone, the implication is I should feel honoured, he can look at a woman sometimes and be so turned on that he just, you know, lets it all go…

I'm sat in the back, in the dark, tired, dying to get home and now I'm sad. He tries to turn into a cycling path.

That's OK though cos he's on a roll. Why would he apologize for driving badly? He doesn't see the cyclist, he's in the middle of telling me more about how he wants to buy a yacht and that's always been his dream, but when he did have money, cos he did have lots of money before his breakdown, he didn't buy one because he was seeing all his girlfriends and having sex with them.

His wife found out. Yeah he's got children, but his ex girlfriend has forgiven him now.

When we get to my home, he tells me how much he's enjoyed the journey. He lingers. He stays outside the house for slightly too long as I go in.

I don't bother to tell anyone.

Women don't bother to tell anyone a lot.

My friend went to the same nail bar in our town for three years. She would always ring up to make an appointment, but every time she went she wondered why they were never ready for her. Turned out she had been ringing one shop for an appointment, and then going to the other nail bar in town to have her nails done. For three years.

KAREN – HAYCROFT

If someone is telling a particularly detailed or exhaustive anecdote, when they've finished I will turn to the person nearest to me and say, 'And that's how I came to marry your grandmother'.

HUW – MERTHYR TYDFIL

'Scrimshanker'. It means someone who does 'just enough', but never anything beyond the call of duty.

SARA

My grandad put on 'Watership Down' when I was five and my sister was three, thinking it was a cute film about rabbits. I still remember the field of blood and the sprint of my nan to the video player.

ANONYMOUS

My first-date dining disaster involved a whole trout. Big mistake. I'd never had it before, and I sawed through the whole lot as if it was a piece of cheese on toast, crunching through mouthfuls of bones, etc.

WENDY – TENBY

DRESS UP

IAN

communication device

M**b**h Tie

cookie

home beard

work beard

marbles

view-master

bubbles

Christian Louboutin Bruno Zip shoes

Bag End key (borrowed)

multi-purpose staff

JO FROST

I AN DISTRACTED BY EVERYTHING

so under rated the pissed off to america...

a genuine force for good

Thank you Jo Frost. I don't have children but I'm surrounded by them, you've helped me a LOT

Propless Panto

No wonder the director is having a tantrum, his dress rehearsal is not going well and his cast have lost or misplaced their props. The stage manager has walked out so it's your chance to step in and help them to get their act together by reuniting the characters with the 'proper props'. There are 13 props to locate.

I love a man who looks like they laugh a lot ... him in The Great Escape ... living in a caravan in The Rockford Files: nice to old people & solving crime ... I bought it completely

JAMES GARNER

Cleaning out my eighty-seven-year-old mum's kitchen drawer, I have found nine potato peelers. She lives on her own.

SAM – LOWESTOFT

I'm currently watching my husband straddle the stairs to apply filler in his skinny jeans. Not the best workwear but the views aren't too bad.

LISA

When I was a student nurse in the early 80s, I unlocked my Ford Escort MK1, climbed in and looked in the rear view mirror. My first thought was 'I don't wear a trilby' – it was resting in the car's rear window. My car was parked further down the road . . .

SUSAN – ORKNEY

Last Christmas my mum was puzzled by my text saying I was icing the circuits. It should have said biscuits.

DEBORAH

I was obsessed with a children's book called 'Mummy Laid an Egg', which explained the birds and the bees in simple terms and funny drawings. I kept it under my bed, and looked at it nightly feeling very guilty . . .

ANONYMOUS

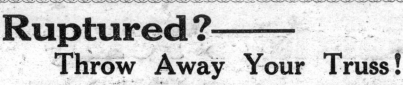

The amount of times old comics went into routines about trusses ... I'd laugh along as a kid, not knowing what the heck a truss was ... The whole world must've been plagued by hernias *

* another reason for me for Time Travelling. You're welcome

WARNING

The next pages contain the stuff of my childhood nightmares. I didn't sleep much.

Haunted by this all my life. It's not a woman's leg but that of a man called Dr John Irving Bentley. I wonder if he was heading for the loo, or had just been...

The Yetis from 'Dr Who'

I must've watched 'Dr Who' with my elder sister. I would dream of these creatures chasing me on a spaceship or jumping up and down on a blue trampoline. It's how I knew I dreamed in colour.

The Child Catcher from 'Chitty Chitty Bang Bang'

Classic and intentional fearmonger, what a great job Robert Helpmann did. He was originally a ballet dancer, and this natural grace added a key sinister quality to his performance.

The rats wrapping Tom Kitten in dough from 'The Roly-Poly Pudding' by Beatrix Potter.

What were these idiots thinking? He's still alive, with fur on...

The Ghost of Christmas Future from 'Scrooge'

The reveal at the graveside, where we can't see the ghost's face, caused me to scream the cinema down. Mum had to take me out.

The Bear from 'The Singing Ringing Tree'

Everything from this East German series gripped me. It was so 'other'...

Ships out of Water

Always eerie because they're so unexpectedly big; it's the iceberg scenario essentially. We used to play on a harbour in Spain when Mum and Dad were having dinner nearby...the dark fed my fears.

The Atom Bomb

Oh the idea of 'the bomb' had me awake for years... I felt it might be up to me to get the cellar ready, but Mum was rather casual about the whole thing.

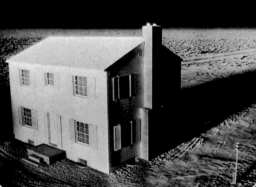

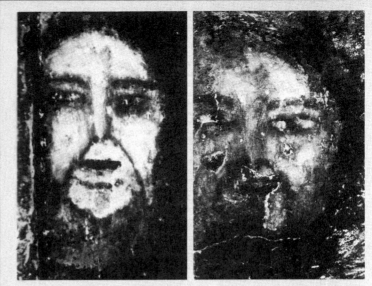

These are just two of the mysterious Faces of Bélmez—the one on the left probably that of a woman. These and other human faces began to appear on the kitchen-floor tiles of a cottage in Spain in 1971. Despite a most exhaustive scientific inquiry no one has ever been able to supply a completely satisfactory natural explanation.

The Faces of Belmez, 'Readers Digest' June 1962

My Grandad Barney taught me to read and used to lend me books that he thought I'd find interesting. I used to dare myself to open this page and look at the faces. Shivery pleasure.

Ragetty from 'The Rupert Bear Annual' 1969

In my mind he was made of birch tree twigs but felt like a bat's skin... he was probably under my bed though... a lot.

A Tapeworm

How did they know I DIDN'T have one.

The murderous Mr. Hyde was portrayed by Fredric March in 1932.

Two people capture the party spirit

I think I was as scared by Yul Brynner in 'Westworld' as I was by the shark in 'Jaws'.

I'd like to write a list of the men I've found to be disappointingly small ... disappointingly short ... but I fear it's a little rude.

I've been thinking about rocking chairs, that whole rocking motion being a comfort. were they invented for nursing mothers or lonely old people who needed a cuddle?

My husband enlightened me regarding the switch in the dining room. Apparently it turns the pump on for the water feature in the garden. Obviously.

NICOLE

My mum took her wig off at the wig counter and tried another one on when I was five. I didn't even know she wore a wig.

RUSTY – CROYDON

Way back in the 70s our budgie landed in my dad's bowl of rice pudding, which had been put aside for his tea when he got back from work. My mum served it up to him.

GILLIAN – YORKSHIRE

My step-mum doesn't do food hygiene. The muddling up of implements, dropping and retrieving, dribbling etc., pale somewhat alongside the ever-present cigarette in her mouth, the ash from which garnishes most of her concoctions. This is always justified by the words, 'you'll eat a ton of (bleep) before you die'.

INSPECTOR MORSEL

Many years ago I dressed as the Mad Hatter for the last night before our badminton hall was to be demolished. Top hat, tails, etc., and a huge plastic carrot. The morning after, my sister, unaware of this, commented on seeing a large inebriated rabbit in tie and tails staggering down the road.

GARRY – CHELMSFORD

BILL MURRAY

I just like him

1971 Power to the People *John Lennon* strong opener, repetitive as the best mantra's are... Hunter S Thompson commented that this song was "10 years too late" that will have stung John I think.

I'm Finding It Harder To Be A Gentleman *The White Stripes* love 'em
John Peel sesh?   multi talented

Laughing At Life *(Take 1) Billie Holliday* AKA Eleonora Fagan... Genius OBV
no idea where I trawled for this track

♥ ♥
♥ Memphis Soul Stew *King Curtis* An all time fave for me, the 'build' cannot fail to
♥ rouse me to mooooove... confident, celebratory, I'm ALIVE ..... King C. did the Sax on
Yakety Yak
INTO
Spreading Honey *The Watts 103rd St Rhythmn Band*
works as a ~~league~~ for me, cools you down but keeps the mood cool & amazing
a generous track
'64 Come See About Me *The Supremes* Diana Ross, Florence Ballard & Mary Wilson,
follow on from 'Baby Love' celebrating all things feminine, offering polish &
nobility - worldwide success

'72 Feel the Need in Me *The Detroit Emeralds*
re released as a disco track in 77

2001 My Friend *Groove Armada* Celetia Martin's vocals; old ravers friend

'72 Walk on the Wild Side *Lou Reed* wore my 'Transformer' LP out... Produced by
David Bowie & Mick Ronson... Bass line ecstasy
risque lyrics slipped past the BBC .... still ....

'58? Twilight Time *Platters* Gorgeous frankly... timed in list to hit twilight
& thrill someone out there

When I'm Gone *Brenda Holloway*
smokey Rob written song... Mary Wells left creating the oppo for Brenda H. to be pushed forward...
Similar to "My Guy" really
Two Headed Woman *Junior Wells* ·record company capitalising
Skillful & Bluesy, a Chicago trait, Great sound

Peanut Butter *The Marathons* Quirky for tea time. this band were called The Vibrations
Good ender.   & The Jay Hawk's too

'58 I Wonder Why *Dion* doo wop classic 'teen angel' B side

I'll Tell My Ma *The Clancy Brothers* Don't think I got to play it.
Big 60's group, part of the US Irish folk boom, sea shanties (♥)
rebel songs & drinking songs. Big influence on Bob Dylan... live sets in N.Y.C.
A line of brothers in hot Aran Jumpers...

The actual selection of tunes to pick from for the end of hour, dependant on mood & time avail.

HANNIBAL HEYES AND
'KID' CURRY

was essentially pure indoctrination in retro.

fancied them both, always loved a cowboy but that

SOUNDS GOOD 3

Read the story and fill in the blanks from the choices below.

Forty-seven-year-old Val Taylor sat in front of her therapist wondering where her tears had gone. For months she not stopped crying; so much so that she had taken to wearing false eyelashes in the daytime to hide her swollen eyes. The one benefit of this was people kept telling her how fabulous she looked. It seemed she had caught up with the compliments.

The therapist smiled at her. 'Did you expect to cry?'

'Yeah.'

'Don't worry, you will.'

They both laughed.

Val sighed. 'I gave all our Christmas decorations to the charity shop this morning. As I was handing over the box, _____ were singing _____ on the stereo and I broke down. The lady made me a cup of tea. It's all just so sad. You don't notice change when you're in it, do you? Well you do, but you choose to ignore it. For years I would sing _____ by_____ to myself, not realizing that I was living the lyrics. The lack of affection for instance.'

'Was it always like that?'

Val thought about their college days and smiled. 'No, far from it. I think we never grew up. Our default setting was as students because that's where we were happiest. "Arrested Development" you called it. We walked down the aisle to _____ by _____.'

'Relationships change, Val, and you had it great for a long time.'

Val welled up, 'I know. I just thought we would be like that _____ song _____.

'Have you started that list?'

Val reached into her bag and pulled out her notebook.

The therapist smiled, 'Things I Want to Do For Me by Val Taylor. Number 1.'

Val took a deep breath.

Music Choices

Chris Montez – The More I See You

Peggy Lee – The Folks Who Live On The Hill

Carole King – Too Late

Fleetwood Mac – Go Your Own Way

The Goons – Unchained Melody

Motorhead – The Ace Of Spades

The Beatles – In My Life

Rolling Stones – Sympathy For The Devil

BRIAN CANT

His 'playschools' were my fave... a wonderfully engaging man. Thank you for everything Mr Cant.

I had to email my staff about changes to their payslips. The spell check auto-corrected payslips to parsnips, I didn't notice and pressed the send button. Only one member of staff spared my blushes and mentioned it. I felt a right old fool!

CATHY – BEXLEYHEATH

Sitting in the garden and wife has performed her normal magic: it's a three course with wine to celebrate a big day for us – we finally paid off our mortgage this morning. Groovy or what?

TROY & SUE – LOWESTOFT

We can't say 'Kawasaki, 'taramasalata' or 'Kodacolor Gold' without saying it in a Geordie accent. HELP.

PAUL & LYNDA – ESSEX

My daughter Jess was given a copy of a Shakespeare play at school and she was delighted to discover the previous student was the amazing Victoria Wood. She passed with flying colours as I am sure Victoria did many years before. The school was Bury Grammar.

JANE – MANCHESTER

What blew my mind at sixteen years old was finding out that Dame Edna was a bloke.

JOHN

The hidden messages in
WATER

WATER IS A FUNDAMENTAL ELEMENT OF LIFE. The average human body is around 70% water, and whilst we could go without food for a number of weeks, every living cell inside our bodies needs water to be able to function.

As with most people I was born with a fascination and respect for water. I'm obsessed with wells and springs, holy, healing or otherwise. My junior school had one of the conduit houses originally built to pump the local water to Hampton Court, and my family home is built on a natural spring with streams running through the garden, above and below ground. Playing at our house usually involved wellies.

I am still driven to clear blocked waterways where I can, and whilst I've always enjoyed these compulsions, I've often felt that I was missing something more spiritual.

Dr Masaru Emoto was a doctor of alternative medicine. He was fascinated by water and in particular its interaction with humans. This might sound far-fetched, but it's also incredibly interesting. Dr Emoto took water samples from all over the world, subjected them to various words or music or electronic devices, and then took photographs of the ice crystals the different waters formed.

Water, he believed, is conscious. It has memory and perception; it's intelligent; it responds to words, whether written or spoken; it reacts to different genres of music;

Distilled water shown the words 'Love and Gratitude'

and it has just been waiting for us to understand this.

Dr Emoto's views are inspiring, the result of a lifetime exploring human wellness. When you've read his books, taking a shower, drinking water, swimming or getting caught in the rain will never be the same. Everything is everything.

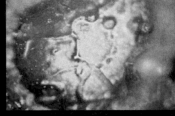

In relation to Dr Emoto's theories, and regarding my own interest in springs and holy wells, did the act of celebrating these sites with prayers of thanks or making token offerings to them as an act of gratitude make the water more potent?

We take water for granted, our ancestors didn't.

Thank you, Dr Emoto.

Lake water before and after a Buddist healing prayer

Thank you (English)

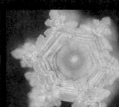
Thank you (Chinese)

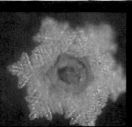
Danke (German)

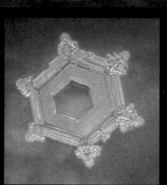
Merci (French)

Thank you (Korean)

Grazie (Italian)

We showed the words meaning 'thank you' in different languages, which then always resulted in crystals that were beautiful and complete

You're Cute

You Fool

Children from an elementary school said different things to bottles of water. When they said 'You're cute' cute cystals formed but 'You fool' had the opposite effect

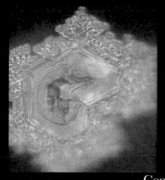

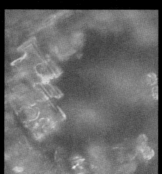
Television

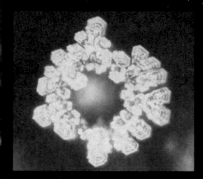
Computer

Samples of distilled water first shown the words 'Love and gratitude' (on the left), then placed next to telivisions and computers (on the right)

The water above is from the Lourdes spring in France and appears similar to crystal formed from water shown the word 'angel'

Taken from the book,
'The Hidden Messages in Water'
by Dr Masaru Emoto

MARINA AND
CAPTAIN TROY TEMPEST

couldn't go swimming without playing I was Aquamarina ... & oh those boy puppets were FAB

If you duck, wouldn't be a pointing index finger? Not sure...

If your hand had to be 'caught' in one pose forever, what would be the most useful? You'd have no real

As an additional precaution he had himself circumcised,

JANUARY
Complete the yearly Accounts. Spare time for sales, and extra entertaining, parties for children and adults. Cleaning the house after Christmas Festivities. Marmalade making.

FEBRUARY
Thorough turning out of all cupboards, shelves, bookcases, chests, in readiness for Spring Cleaning.

MARCH
Early Spring Cleaning, interior decorating, upholstery, making curtains, chair covers.

APRIL
Spring Cleaning, washing curtains, preparing for Easter. Spring gardening.

MAY
Late Spring Cleaning. Attend to outhouses. Spring Clean the garage, tool-sheds. Clean and put away winter clothes. Protect from moth. Gardening. Bedding out. Window boxes.

JUNE
Preparation and sewing for the holidays. Fruit bottling.

JULY
Jam making. Fruit and vegetable bottling. Holidays.

AUGUST
Preserving. Sewing. Buy winter coal. Holidays.

SEPTEMBER
Making pickles and sauces. Plum and Damson jam. Getting in winter stores when needed.

OCTOBER
Harvesting of Vegetables. Packing away summer clothes. Launder or send away to be cleaned. Renovate the wardrobe. Unpack winter clothes and furs. Inspect the outside of the house and carry out any small repairs.

NOVEMBER
Preparing Christmas Puddings, Mincemeat, Cakes. Christmas Shopping.

DECEMBER
Making and buying Christmas Presents. Christmas Cooking and Letter Writing. Overhauling children's wardrobe when they come home for holidays.

ACHTUNG

Memory game ahead

On the next pages are 30 objects. Look at them for 1 minute, close the book and try to remember as many as you can.

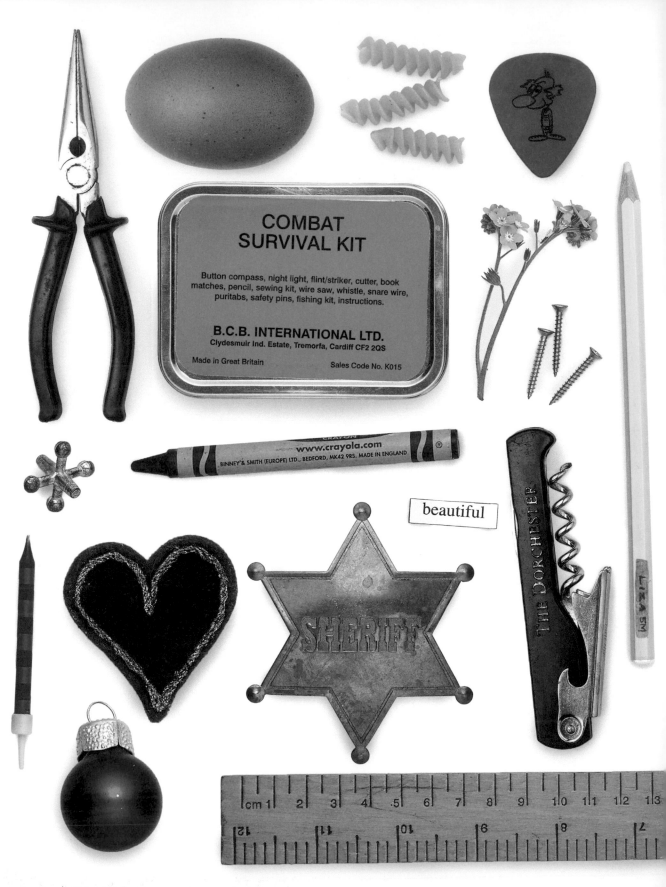

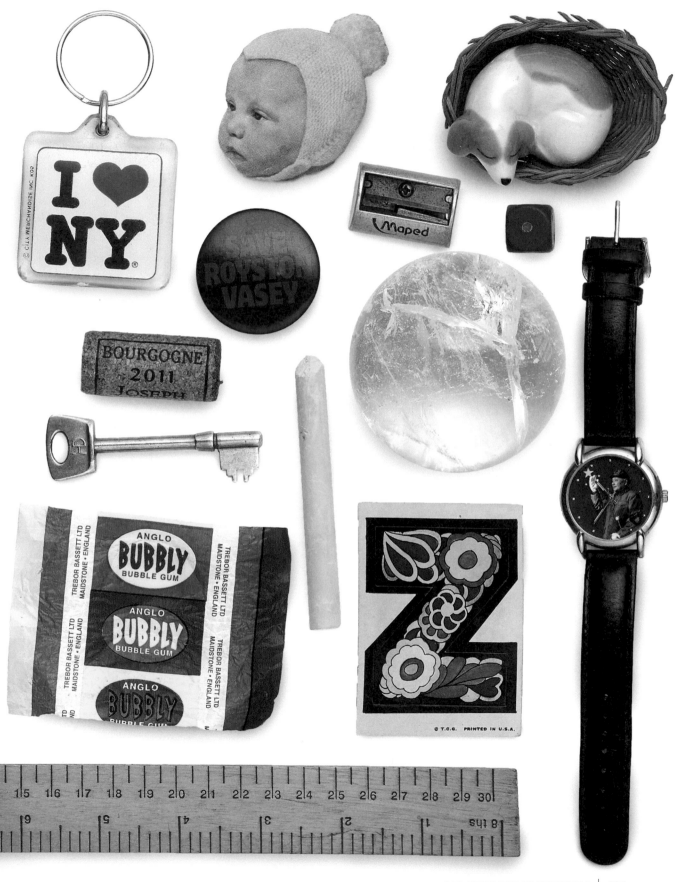

Tonight we won't be eating pulled pork after just discovering our fourteen-year-old son unplugged the slow cooker five hours ago to make toast.

ANONYMOUS

The foam filling of an old pouf burst out five years ago. We've left it on the living room floor for five years like a dead animal.

BEN – BARNET

When I'm in the shop buying 'loose' vegetables or fruit I always feel guilty when I choose one avocado or potato over another. I always (quietly) apologize to the other veg and fruit, excusing myself for leaving them behind, nothing personal, etc.

HEATHER – GLASGOW

It seems the D of E just gets harder and harder. All I had to do to get my bronze was to crochet a beer mat.

BAZ – BRUM

My wife ordered a pair of glasses and two picture frames in the same week. She received a phone call saying that there was a big problem with the frames, and could they make them larger, with bigger glass. 'How will that work', she asked, 'won't they be too big for my face?' The caller replied, 'Don't worry, we will make the wooden frames larger too'. 'WOODEN! I haven't ordered wooden glasses'. It was the picture framers calling.

DAVID

There was an uncomfortable silence.

Desiderata

Go placidly amid the noise and haste,
and remember what peace there may be in silence.
As far as possible, without surrender,
be on good terms with all persons.
Speak your truth quietly and clearly;
and listen to others,
even to the dull and ignorant;
they too have their story.

Avoid loud and aggressive persons,
they are vexatious to the spirit.
If you compare yourself with others,
you may become vain and bitter,
for always there will be greater and lesser
persons than yourself.
Enjoy your achievements
as well as your plans.

Keep interested in your own career,
however humble;
it is a real possession
in the changing fortunes of time.
Exercise caution in your business affairs,
for the world is full of trickery.
But let this not blind you to what virtue there is;
many persons strive for high ideals,
and everywhere life is full of heroism.
Be yourself.

Especially do not feign affection.
Neither be cynical about love;
for in the face of all aridity and disenchantment it is
as perennial as the grass.
Take kindly the counsel of the years,
gracefully surrendering the things of youth.
Nurture strength of spirit to shield you
in sudden misfortune.
But do not distress yourself with dark imaginings.
Many fears are born of fatigue and loneliness.

Beyond a wholesome discipline,
be gentle with yourself.
You are a child of the universe
no less than the trees and the stars;
you have a right to be here.
And whether or not it is clear to you,
no doubt the universe is unfolding as it should.

Therefore be at peace with God,
whatever you conceive Him to be.
And whatever your labors and aspirations,
in the noisy confusion of life,
keep peace with your soul.
With all its sham, drudgery and broken dreams,
it is still a beautiful world.
Be cheerful.
Strive to be happy.

MAX EHRMANN

Around 1980 I was working as a pot washer in a well-known local 'banqueting suite'. They served a sorbet course consisting of lemon sorbet on top of a fancy carved lemon. After the course, the plates would arrive at the pot wash, chucked through the hatch with the leftover gravy, peas, chicken bones, used napkins, etc., and we would have to sort the lemons out because they were re-used. One night we had a lemon fight. They were stuck to us, the walls, the floor, ceiling, etc. When the supervisor stuck her head round the door and shouted, 'I hope you've kept them lemons!' We collected them all, and because they were a bit grubbier than usual we put them through the dishwasher. They came out a bit pale, but were probably more hygienic than they had been for weeks. No-one died, but I've never eaten lemon sorbet since.

KOJAK

Heard on a bus: 'Don't talk to me about cucumbers, what my husband does with cucumbers you can't imagine!' I tried not to imagine, but I couldn't help myself.

CHRIS – NORTHUMBERLAND

I have a customer who has a whole home cinema hidden up in his loft – his wife is completely unaware of its existence or how many £1000s it cost. He only uses it when she's out at bingo!

ANDY – TOLLESHUNT D'ARCY

My wife Yvonne has some bridge event tonight, so I am home alone. As a surprise for her I'm making bread (fully clothed) and have just started my first rise. Hopefully I can get a second rise before she gets back home.

MICK

DRESS UP
PATRICIA

yoyo

swanee
whistle

dart

PAT vs.

20
19
18
17
16
15
8

dartboard

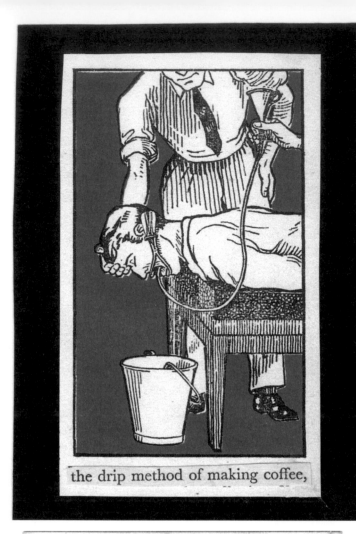

the drip method of making coffee,

This creature was killed in 1920 along the Colombia-Venezuela border. Unlike any monkey known from South America, it was, claimed its discoverer, five feet tall and tailless.

THE BARK AND FLOWERS OF CINCHONA.

DO YOU KNOW what Quinine is ?

The curative qualities of quinine were first discovered by the Indians of S. America, one of whom is said to have cured a Jesuit missionary of fever by means of it. The Jesuits introduced the medicine into Europe, where it became generally known as Jesuits' bark, Peruvian bark, or Cinchona. It is now largely cultivated in S. America, India, and Java, which are the chief sources of the world's supply of quinine. The trees are uprooted when they contain the maximum amount of the drug, and their bark stripped. In India the bark is sometimes only partially removed, and allowed to grow again. Quinine is an invaluable medicine in tropical countries.

Chart your life story via the perfume* that you wore. From the first bottle you bought to the one you wear now....

* or aftershave

Bloody Nora, he's gor it...

STEVE MCQUEEN

I AN DISTRACTED BY EVERYTHING today it's been bums. Babies bums, bums in jeggings, dogs bums.

cheesy puffs · starry nights · jelly · almonds · sheds · paper · cat kind · depth · silk · shopping lists · ponies cherry red · flavour · courage · chops · kids on bikes · India · circles figs · ghost stories · common sense · watching people paddling · shade · knitters · a massage · treasure hunting · fishing · bowls · sausages · elephants baubles · snow badgers · glitter · waves · magic · copper · lego · rice krispies · pickles · wine · dancing buttons · spag bol · blue plaques conditioner · comedians · portugal · curators bridges · pedicures · a wash of logs · a sharp knife lollipops code · family wit · ribbons · fish tanks truculent youth · synchronicity · buds · a double yolker · cauliflower cheese · noodles maps · holding bathed babies · greenery · Scrabble bellinis · refreshment · clear thinking · good lyrics · dogs in sunbeams · moonlight · bright ideas · impulses · kissing bar-b-q's harps · distant mountains · resonance trumpets chips budgies · old school glamour · great drums · being charmed pop socks · my dressmaker · knees birch ply · clean windows cards · satisfaction · natas · old front doors · dolls houses · grass · pompons english · floorplans · action · mulberries pigs · feeling excited · a mattress topper · understanding · social history · drunk laughing planting coloured pencils · a great plan · sans old churches · secret passages · the phoenicians · spain blossom · ebay · snap dragons · gaffer tape · france · chiffon puffers hammocks GiGi's · oysters · stripes · rainbows · professionalism · spelling a word · night · curry · moongates · metaphysics · castles · radio · jars · campfires · caves · fresh mint · promise · lustre · wellies · dogs feet · journeying · a singalong shadows · etchings · hedgerows · meadows · guiness · leis · black cats · geegaws · a hot shower · swimming in the sea · salad · fresh flowers

Bright 'n' beady
tea cosy

*The wonderful **Minky Whale** inspires you to refresh and recycle*

I found myself with a plethora of sturdy cloth shopping bags and decided to put one to good use by updating my faded tea cosy cover. This is basic sewing, it's not difficult, and the beauty is in the embellishments.

Grab one of your cloth bags and lay it flat, then take the tea cosy padding and draw around it, leaving a good inch or two beyond your line for shrinkage or errors.
Cut the shape out, and then, following the line you drew, sew the two pieces together. Trim all excess.

If you haven't got a machine, it's perfectly possible to sew this by hand.

Be generous with the hem and turn it up (no need to sew) so that it fits perfectly over the padding.

Select the fabric you want to use, and cut into smallish circles. I used a little jar to get the shape.

When you have enough circles to cover your base, start arranging them in a way that pleases you.

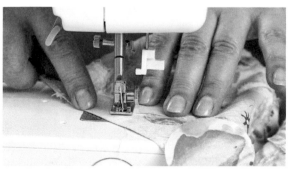

Start sewing them on. I machined mine on, and you don't have to be careful, because you can hide anything unsightly with beads later on.

You may want to mix up your textures and sew a few of the prettier circles on by hand.

Time to start beading.

I find proper beading needles a must for this job; they may be flimsier, but if you're using tiny beads, you can load the needle with several beads at a time. This will be useful, as beading can ruin your bloody eyesight.

I have ruined my eyesight.

DAVID BOWIE

other worldly GENIUS has my total respect as a creative thinker totally classy totally love him. I think of him at least once a day. Really.

I knew someone who bought a second-hand book from a charity shop whilst on holiday in the UK and his actual class photo (age thirteen) was in it, having been used as a bookmark.
He was fifty-seven at the time.

CHRISTINE

I'm suffering from pickled lip syndrome. I pickled a batch of turnips with beetroot a couple of weeks ago and I've almost finished the lot! My lips are as white as snow!

JEAN – SOMERSET

One of my favourite pieces of graffiti was on a brick wall on the way to Victoria Park in East London just saying 'I miss her'. So melancholy and reflective.

MELVYN – EAST FINCHLEY

Tom's wearing shoes with holes in the toes for the next five weeks of term. He needs to learn to use the brakes on his bike.

CHARLEY – RUGBY

Could you please wish my wife Ruth a happy wedding anniversary from me? To be honest she's quite the lucky lady as I am a bit of a catch.

MARK

The funniest thing we saw when looking for a house was a Yorkshire Terrier following us from room to room with a sausage in its mouth.

ANDREA – STAFFORDSHIRE

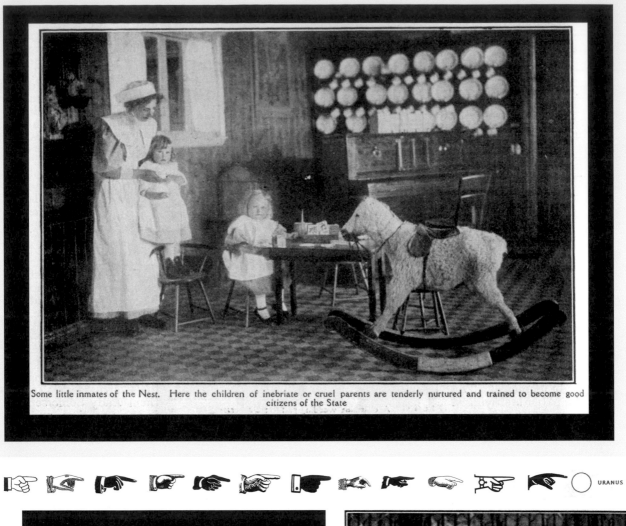

Some little inmates of the Nest. Here the children of inebriate or cruel parents are tenderly nurtured and trained to become good citizens of the State

URANUS

Listen dear, I know it's been difficult for you lately, and I thought it might be a good idea to send you away for a while.

The jerboa is a particularly suitable pet for a lady, being of a gentle and confiding disposition and engaging ways

HEEL-AND-TOE WALKING
TECHNIQUE

I had a weird celebrity dream over Christmas. I was sitting on a communal loo next to Jeremy Clarkson, and he was crafting a birthday card using a dead mouse as decoration. He wanted me to admire it, but I was just desperate for a wee.

KAREN

I too had a Clarkson toilet dream this week. He was dressed as Henry VIII.

MAGNUM PI – TAMWORTH

I have to put my right sock on then my left sock, my right shoe then my left shoe. I always start with my right foot or it feels odd.

CARLENE

When choosing a purchase (plant, toy, gift) I cannot pick any of the items up before buying, because I cannot put it back as I have got its hopes up and it thinks it has been chosen to come home with us.

LOUISE – KENT

On holiday I always take a bar of non-perfumed soap with me, and I have a strange need to bring it back rather than leave it in the hotel. Not because I'm mean, but because I feel guilty leaving behind something that has come all the way from home with us; 'Mr Soap' is like a friend of the family.

MICK – SHEFFIELD

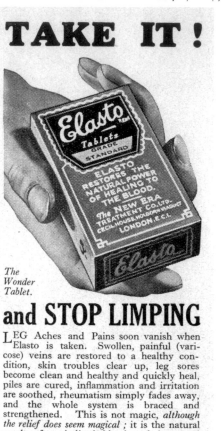

TAKE IT !

The Wonder Tablet.

and STOP LIMPING

LEG Aches and Pains soon vanish when Elasto is taken. Swollen, painful (varicose) veins are restored to a healthy condition, skin troubles clear up, leg sores become clean and healthy and quickly heal, piles are cured, inflammation and irritation are soothed, rheumatism simply fades away, and the whole system is braced and strengthened. This is not magic, *although the relief does seem magical ;* it is the natural result of revitalised blood and improved circulation brought about by Elasto, *the tiny tablet with wonderful healing powers.*

Elasto Will Save You Pounds

The " Story of Elasto " is the title of an interesting booklet which explains in simple language the Elasto method of curing through the blood. Your copy is free, see offer below. Suffice it to say here that Elasto restores to the blood the vital elements which combine with the blood albumin to form organic elastic tissue and thus enables *Nature* to restore elasticity to the broken-down and devitalised fabric of veins, arteries, and heart and so to re-establish normal circulation, *the real basis of sound health !* Elasto is prepared in tiny tablets *which dissolve instantly* on the tongue, and it is the pleasantest, the cheapest, and the most effective remedy ever devised. For the outlay of a few shillings you can now enjoy the tremendous advantages of this Modern Scientific remedy, which has cost thousands of pounds to perfect.

What Users of Elasto Say—

" No sign of varicose veins now."
" Elasto has quite cured my Eczema."
" Now walk long distances with ease."
" My heart is quite sound again now."
" Completely cured my varicose ulcers."
" Now free from Piles."
" Cured my rheumatism and neuritis."

You Can Test Elasto Free !

Simply send your name and address, without delay to : ELASTO (Dept. 11 A.), Cecil House, Holborn Viaduct, London, E.C., and your Free Sample and Free Booklet, telling you all about Elasto, will reach you by return post. You will soon be saying, as thousands of others have already said—" I wish I had known of Elasto before." Send NOW, while you think of it. This offer is too good to be missed.

Issued by The New Era Treatment Co., Ltd.

[vertical handwritten note, left margin] I love early adverts; no mention of what's actually in it, but because it says so in black and white it must be true... we've been fools

[vertical printed text] **auspicious** promising success, favoured by good fortune, prosperous

The Firewood Poem

Beechwood fires are bright and clear
If the logs are kept a year.
Chestnut's only good they say,
If for logs 'tis laid away.
Make a fire of Elder tree,
Death within your house will be;
But ash new or ash old,
Is fit for a queen with crown of gold

Birch and fir logs burn too fast
Blaze up bright and do not last.
It is by the Irish said
Hawthorn bakes the sweetest bread.
Elm wood burns like churchyard mould,
E'en the very flames are cold.
But ash green or ash brown,
Is fit for a queen with golden crown

Poplar gives a bitter smoke,
Fills your eyes and makes you choke.
Apple wood will scent your room
Pear wood smells like flowers in bloom.
Oaken logs, if dry and old
keep away the winter's cold.
But ash wet or ash dry,
a king shall warm his slippers by.

by Celia Congreve

[vertical handwritten note, right margin] I went & cut hazel twigs new at Tarby Towers to replace any bamboo supports in my garden & the result was astonishing, thank you Sarah Raven, nothing to distract the eye from the plants... well

[handwritten note, top margin] saw that, but I didn't realise how much the vertical rods dcew down my eye.

208

IS THERE ANY RULE about women being able to make their Communion when not wearing a hat?

For many centuries it has been the custom that women should wear hats at public gatherings, and especially in church, but this is (or was) a custom, not a law, and customs may be changed by general consent. Archbishop Temple made it clear that there was no ecclesiastical objection to women appearing hatless in church, and in so doing he was merely confirming what had, in fact, become a widespread use.

**Ten characters (not including the Fab Four)
seen on the Sergeant Pepper's album cover...** **GO**

[handwritten note, bottom] I wonder if ~~some~~ somewhere down the line Harry Potter isn't John Lennon. Discuss.

Spit the Dofference

Can you spot the twelve differences between these two pictures?

Iʼve just read that Londonʼs old pipes were made of elm, for all the good it did them

Stylish Snippets

funny terms

Cankles
an ankle that blends into a calf or a calf that blends into an ankle?

◆

Rag and boner
when you more than love a fashion item

◆

Lampshading
an oversized top worn with a fitted lower half

◆

Whorts
winter shorts to be worn with tights

◆

Chi chi
over fancy, showy or pretentious

◆

Shoots
in between a shoe and a boot

◆

Shacket
can be pronounced ssshhhacket: a shirt/jacket

BEST PHYSIQUE FOR APRIL

COMPETITION FOR MEN ONLY

South African Reader, *Leonard Rice, winner of the April Competition.*

All male readers are invited to submit photographs of themselves for the monthly Best Physique Competition. A Cash Prize of £1 1 0 will be awarded each month to the picture which, in the opinion of the Editor, shows the most pleasing male physique. Muscular poses taken indoors will be considered but readers should endeavour to produce a pleasing—rather than a muscular—pose. Photographs of the nude figure must be retouched before they are sent through the post. Name and address must accompany each photograph, and while we are prepared to return all unused pictures accompanied by a stamped addressed envelope, we cannot guarantee it. Mark your photos: Best Physique Competition, Health & Efficiency, and send them to the Editor, Health & Efficiency, 4-8, Greville St., Holborn, London, E.C.1. The Editor reserves the right to publish any of the photographs submitted free of charge.

As this issue closed for press on May 10th the May Competition result will be published in the next issue.

"*Health & Efficiency,*" 4-8, *Greville St., Holborn, London, E.C.1*

Subtlety can be delicious, itʼs often the juice a joke floats in. So when someone says, ʻDid you see what I did there?ʼ it makes me want to punch them.

WRESTLING
SENSATIONAL MAIN EVENT
★★★★★★★★★
PHILIP **GLASS** vs
CHAS **SMASH**
SPECIAL GUEST
PAUL MICHAEL GLASER

Cor means heart in Latin

1972 Superstition Stevie Wonder _Musicians have by necessity to be generous but some go into consummate Toff territory Mr W. is one. Jeff Beck started the drum beat, inspired Stevie to riff over it... TOOUUUNNE!_

wrong word sussed? An old pro basically

Everybody Eats When They Come To My House Cab Calloway _Cab Calla... his whole energy feels tight but easy, used to performing live... Great 2nd track..._

1967 Soul Man Sam & Dave _written by Isaac Hayes & David Porter... 2 versions with different intro's, classic 'pride' track._

1969 By A Waterfall The Bonzo Dog Band - _pesky art school boys messing with our minds from the Album 'Tadpoles'_

1958 The Stripper David Rose & Orchestra _This is just a phenominal bit of music for me, why is it funny? Indecent trombones & rude trumpers. Briefly married to Judy Garland_

2012 Default Django Django _freshens this list up, more art school fellas_

You've Got the Love Florence & The Machine _Class rework of an '86 Candi Staton, commitment, intent & an eye for detail... Polished_

Rat Race The Specials _go through their catalogue all year... 2 tone/ska hold memories for my era as it burst into the psyche... Elvis Costello produced their debut album... love Terry Hall dour git_

Hang On Sloopy Quincy Jones _The McCoys had the first connotation of this track Dorothy Sloop was a Jazz pianist classy easy track, another GENIUS_

Dat Dere Oscar Brown Jnr _A favourite of mine, flat remastering of his tracks infuriate me. This is a bit 'cute' & I've overplayed it in my 20's, BUT he's rare & well produced... fits great with the next track..._

1967 Lovely Rita The Beatles _SGT. Pepper classic.... transposes Oscar B's cute into something else... similar intent ??_

1972 Lady Stardust David Bowie _Is this about Marc Bolan?_

Something's Coming Carol Lawrence _Refresh/Reset, with a good show tune. → Musical theatre legend._

1974 I Can't Stand the Rain Ann Peebles _Both Ian Drury & John Lennon cited this as a fave track... electric timbale providing attention grabbing intro... classic_

Oo-de-Lally Roger Miller _end of hour, see what mood we're in for a quick track to end, I like Rogers easy vibe. similar voice to Johnny Cash actually..._

61 I Love How You Love Me The Paris Sisters _classic little teenage favourite... got that 'talcy' softness..._

Phil Spector produced

yes, it's HALF 2, & I've a tonne of things to do...

ALASTAIR SIM

I love him with Margaret Rutherford ... but what an actor & what a voice ...

Whenever I hear someone beep their horn I always say, 'Who's tootin' who?' in a sort of American 1940's detective style. My husband hates it. Makes it all the more pleasurable to say.

LAUREN

Any ten-pin bowler will tell you that dishwashers were invented to wash bowling balls.

BILLY – COUNTY DURHAM

I was trying to glue a small pearl back on to my earring and managed to stick my left thumb and first finger to my right thumb and first finger. I was living alone, it was 10.30pm and I had undone my jeans (for comfort). I had to get my neighbours Flo and Bernie out of their bed to free me.

CHRISSIE – NORTHAMPTON

I can't say 'power shower' without a Northern Irish accent.

SARAH – HEREFORDSHIRE

Being the youngest of three children, by quite a few years, I always had to go to bed first, but was always comforted that my mum told me that everyone else followed shortly after. Imagine the shock I had after waking up in the dark to hear laughing coming from the living room downstairs. I crept down and opened the door quietly to see my parents, brother and sister sitting by the fire, playing cards and eating toast. They all looked at me and I knew that they knew they had been rumbled, big time. Still remember that feeling. Never mind, I have made them pay, for a long time.

CATHY

does this book qualify as a feminine lexicon?

Casting thoughts...

Words I always have to check the spelling of:
rhythm
conscience
necessary
yacht
psychic
Milieu

never argue for your limitations. I would have done it BUT, I tried to do it BUT, I'm sorry I'm late BUT... you are exactly where you're meant to be

Ten things that Ian Drury thinks are reasons to be cheerful... go

Guess whose facial hair
ARTISTS
① ② ③
④ ⑥
⑤

Temporary is always longer than you think

One of the hardest parts of getting organized is having to be being present during the process.

Why have we been given fathomless emotional abilities, if what we feel about something, isn't more important than what we think about it...?

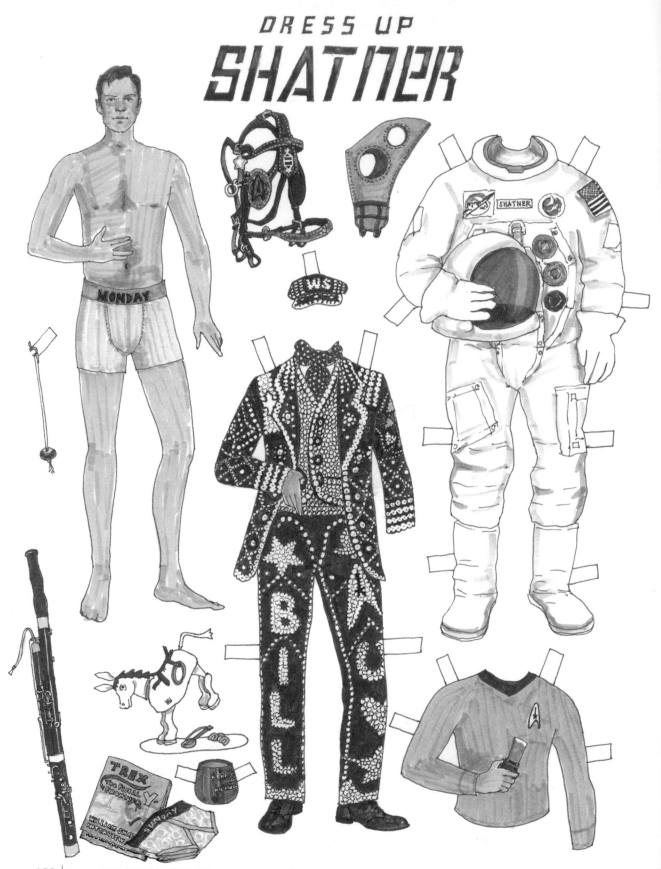

Sometimes a mood just keeps showing itself within an hour, I can see I've put a couple in this hour to pep up the energy, but it's clear I can't fight it's laid back feel; I think this was a winter list, it's just got that "take it easy" it's dark out shoon. I like it though.

Mr Kicks — Oscar Brown Jnr
Dream opener for me, properly different from show before mine. Grabs attention... from original un remastered 'Heaven and Hell' Album. hard to find.

We Open in Venice — The Rat Pack
Good 2nd track, Showy & high, suitably camp & a memory of a dear friend

How Glad I Am — Fontella Bass
Gospel background. I adore Fontella. This song is pure gold... could've had Nancy Wilson but I suspect I was saving her for the next hour...

Am I the Man — Jackie Wilson
not the obvious JW track, but he's a great tether at this point in the list. Great push, confident & fun

Hero — Family of the Year
freshen-up-erer... wonderfully haunting, clean & clear lovely builder, feels good

1976 I Love to Boogie — T.Rex
Geeing us up again, familiarity after a new song... controversial when released, it's so like a Webb Pierce song, there's a whole programme in that musical plagerism...

1978 Love Is in the Air — John Paul Young
worldwide hit, fabulous, an easy pleaser

75/76 Midnight Rider — Paul Davidson
my fave version I think an easy skank

So What — Ronny Jordan
In for variation, classy version & I'm a RJ fan, I like an instrumental shoved in, as long as it's worth it!! Long though, that hard in the middle but it's the guitar riff that thrills me essentially (of its time)

2003 released 2011 Our Day Will Come — Amy Winehouse
Intended to be off "Frank", not sure why it never made it, it's wonderful... makes you miss her

1969 Pinball Wizard — The Who
old classic, one for the boys(?) — quickly written & recorded, it's got that 'unfiddled' with flavour... don't mind it...

1981 It Must Be Love — Madness (1971)
oh how I LOVE this track, will usually need the Labi Siffri orig. but sometimes I want the Nutty Boys. as I doff my cap to them finding it reworking it & letting us enjoy big butch fellas sing about love

Moonlight Saving Time — Blossom Dearie
I adore Blossom... this is lovely and bouncy, great scan, always great humour somehow...

1968 Suzanne — Francoise Hardy
fabulous version, good to hear a french lyric, arresting

Moonlight Cocktail — Mel Torme
Glenn Miller tune reworked from "Ripples of the Nile" (Nipples of the Rile?)
lovely & familiar. beautifully handled

(Bet I ended the hour on Suzanne though!)

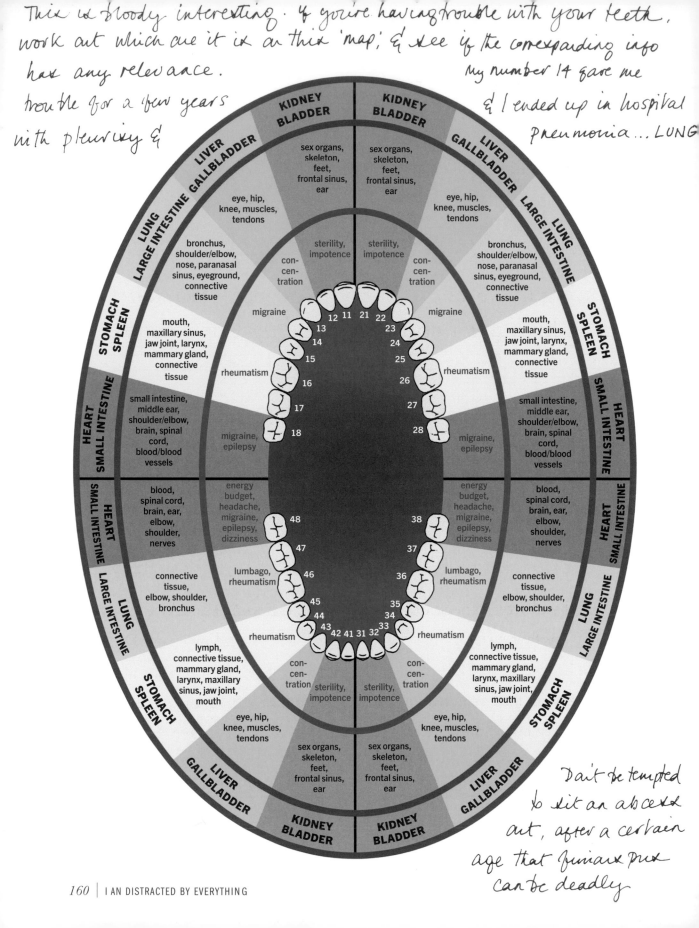

This is bloody interesting. If you're having trouble with your teeth, work out which one it is on this 'map', & see if the corresponding info has any relevance.

trouble for a few years with pleurisy &

My number 14 gave me & I ended up in hospital pneumonia... LUNG

Don't be tempted to sit an abscess out, after a certain age that funny pus can be deadly

My grandad once chopped one of his fingers off in the lawn mower. He bunged it in some salt, then stuck it back together using one of my Nana's curlers for a brace. He used the same method next time he did it.

CLAIRE

Was delighted this Christmas to find, whilst perusing my father's old house maintenance journal, that in his budget costs for installing a new shower in the early 80s he'd allowed for a bottle of Cinzano.

KEN – EDINBURGH

The height of sophistication – Arctic Roll. Not only was it sophisticated, but it also defied the laws of physics. Ice cream in the oven.

KEITH

When I walk alongside another person I always thought it was normal to walk in rhythm with that person until I got with my now fiancée and she confronted me about it a few months into our relationship.

JOE IN THE OFFICE

To differentiate between my brother and my mate Dave, who lived in the fish & chip shop at the top of the street, we called him Fishy Dave. He then got dumped by three consecutive girlfriends. He was renamed Jilted Fish.

STEVE – LEEDS

HATTIE JACQUES AND
ERIC SYKES

fill a whole page with all the things you LOVE about your partner *small writing*

VIVIENNE WESTWOOD

How utterly fabulous can we woman be?

Whilst watching TV my husband Karl gave himself frostbite! He had pulled a muscle at the gym and had put an ice pack on his thigh. He left it on too long and his leg set completely solid like a frozen pork chop. Having Googled what to do, body temperature seemed the best solution. So I had to sit on him. Our teenage sons think we are ridiculous.

DEB – BRENTWOOD

My mum said women of a certain age shouldn't wear beige jackets as from the back they look like a baked potato.

LORNA – EDINBURGH

My wife names all the white goods in the house: the fridge, washing machine, even the dishwasher. Everything has to have a name. I despair.

MARK

When I was little the blinds in the bathroom window, which was opposite my bedroom, looked like the face of Jesus. I quite often had to get out of bed and close the door. I couldn't take the pressure of being watched by somebody so important.

VICKIE – YEOVIL

My mum often thought about her best friend from university, as they lost touch after Mum got married in the late 70s. In 2005, Mum stumbled across an abandoned baggage label on the floor at Heathrow. It had his name, address and phone number on it! Now they are back in touch and the best of friends again. Serendipity?

FIONA – WOKINGHAM

RACE TO

THE TOPPERMOST ★ no **1** ★ **OF THE POPPERMOST**

Here's a fab game where each player becomes **The Beatles** navigating the rocky road to fame and fortune! All you need to play is a coin or a button as a marker. Throw a 6 to start rocking and the race to the Toppermost of the Poppermost is on!

THE LADS RESORT TO AMPHETAMINES TO GET THEM THROUGH THE LONG HOURS OF STAGE TIME. FORWARD 7 SPACES.

15

RINGO INTRODUCES RORY STORM AND THE HURRICANES TO BAKED BEANS, CAUSING THEM TO LIVE UP TO THEIR NAME. BACK 3 SPACES.

THE LADS RETURN FROM HAMBURG WITH MUCH-IMPROVED MUSICAL ABILITY AND SEVERAL UNUSUAL RASHES. FORWARD 4 SPACES.

12

17

THE BEATLES GO TO HAMBURG WITH ONLY ONE PAIR OF PANTS AND A THREEPENNY PIECE BETWEEN THEM. MISS A GO.

NEW DRUMMER PETE BEST LOSES SMILE IN TRAGIC ACCIDENT. BACK 1 SPACE.

21

THE LADS SECURE THEIR FIRST EVER PAID GIG IN A COUSIN'S OUTSIDE TOILET FOR ONE SHILLING AND SIXPENCE. FORWARD 2 SPACES.

23

19

36

RINGO CONTRACTS DIPHTHERIA AGED 5. BACK 3 SPACES.

38

START

Go man GO!

39

2

3

GEORGE MARTIN IGNORES IMPERTINENT TIE JIBE AND OFFERS THE BEATLES A RECORDING CONTRACT. FORWARD 2 SPACES.

5

RINGO JOINS THE GROUP AFTER INSISTING HIS NOSE IS GIVEN ITS OWN CONTRACTUAL PERCENTAGE. FORWARD 2 SPACES.

BRIAN EPSTEIN SEES THE BEATLES AND ADMITS TO HIS PARENTS THAT HIS NATURAL INCLINATION IS NOT TOWARD THE RETAIL SECTOR. TAKE ANOTHER GO.

10

9

JOHN AND PAUL WRITE 87 SONGS IN AN HOUR AND 10 MINUTES. FORWARD 3 SPACES.

DECCA TURN DOWN THE BEATLES SAYING 'GUITAR GROUPS AND EXIT SIGNS ARE ON THE WAY OUT'.

TEDDY BOY RINGO STOPS HITTING PEOPLE AND STARTS HITTING DRUMS. FORWARD 2 SPACES.

THE LADS CHANGE THEIR NAME FROM THE QUARRYMEN TO BLACK LACE. BACK 1 SPACE.

26

THE LADS RECRUIT THE FIRST OF THEIR 74 DRUMMERS BEFORE RINGO. FORWARD 1 SPACE.

PAUL INTRODUCES GEORGE TO JOHN WHO THEN RELIEVES HIM OF HIS DINNER MONEY. MISS A TURN.

JOHN'S SCOTTISH UNCLE BUYS HIM A SET OF BAGPIPES FOR HIS 11TH BIRTHDAY. BACK 1 SPACE.

RINGO CONTRACTS SCARLET FEVER AGED 7. BACK 2 SPACES.

JOHN NOT ONLY WINS THE MEAT RAFFLE AT THE WOOLTON CHURCH FETE BUT IS ALSO INTRODUCED TO PAUL. FORWARD 3 SPACES.

30

33

PAUL WORKS OUT HOW TO PLAY A RIGHT-HANDED GUITAR BACK TO FRONT, UPSIDE DOWN AND STANDING ON HIS HEAD. FORWARD 4 SPACES.

RINGO CONTRACTS BUBONIC PLAGUE AGED 11. BACK 6 SPACES.

JACARANDA CLUB 2 NITE: THE BEATALS

Winners become incredibly rich and famous for the rest of their lives. Losers return to Liverpool to work in a bottling factory and then die early, embittered and in debt.

SOUNDS GOOD 4

Read the story and fill in the blanks from the choices below.

Forty-nine-year-old Val Taylor had got off her face on therapy in one form or another for the past three years. She was (nearly) feeling fabulous. The constant nourishment of friends and family was mending her, although it had taken a while to stop _____ singing _____ on a loop in her head.

On the wobbly morning of (what would have been) her 25th wedding anniversary, Val stood in the queue for the Ladies at Euston Station. _____ sang _____ from the speakers and she watched an angry cleaner mop the floor ferociously. The mop was moving nearer and nearer to her and then all over her boots.

The cleaner glared at her and growled, 'Get out of the way!'

Not in the mood for such rudeness, Val stormed in to the cubicle, furious.

Ten minutes later Val knocked on the supervisor's door. 'Hello. Can I speak to the lady who was just mopping the floor?'

The supervisor stared stony-faced at Val. 'Joan, this woman wants you.'

The cleaner's face appeared at the door. 'What?'

Val Taylor handed her a bunch of tea roses. 'These are for you. You looked like you were having a really bad day. I love a clean toilet and I just wanted to say thanks.'

Joan's face fell to the floor and her eyes welled up with tears, 'I don't know what to say.'

'You don't have to say anything. I just wanted to say thanks.'

The supervisor patted Joan on her back. 'Blimey, Head Office are going to love this.'

Val walked away. One of the things that she'd learnt to do was change her habits. Complaining would have compacted everyone's misery; this way, everyone was touched by a ripple of joy. She put her on her headphones and pressed shuffle. _____ by _____ came on, and the fabulous Val Taylor walked away.

Music Choices

Barry Manilow – Copacabana

Harry Belafonte – The Banana Boat Song

The Crusaders – Street Life

David Bowie – Changes

Dusty Springfield – I Just Don't Know

Cliff Richard – Wired For Sound

Jess Glynne – Hold My Hand

Stevie Wonder – Overjoyed

David Rose Orchestra – The Stripper

Helen Shapiro – Walking Back to Happiness

Dogs were treated as equals ... in our house... well... not quite true.

together ... opening the back door, "Louis, Gundy's here" off they'd go ...

watched three at The Natural History Museum, mum couldn't hear me away... I knew animals were cleverer than they let on. We had a golden Labrador called Louis, his mate (a black lab called Gundy) would call at the back door for him & they'd go

THE INCREDIBLE JOURNEY

Whilst weeding the front garden of our new cottage, we noticed some ornate brickwork at ground level. It looked like the top of a buried window. The only possible entrance to an underground room was a small walk-in cupboard in our kitchen. I borrowed a sledgehammer and whacked a hole into the likeliest cupboard wall. Shining a torch through the hole and brick-dust, I saw a row of steps descending into the gloom. I've never had such an Indiana Jones moment – I squeezed through, scrambled down, and discovered a large, usable cellar. Now when I buy a house and don't discover a secret cellar I feel disappointed.

DAVID

After many years I still say, 'Hold on there, bald eagle' when asking someone to slow down or back up a bit and explain. As this is from the TEXAN Bar advert of probably thirty years ago, no one knows what I am talking about.

STEVE – MONTROSE

My wife went to the hairdressers today and they gave her the barnet of a cockatiel. I find this strangely alluring.

TED – TUNBRIDGE WELLS

After the toast pops up, I always say 'Thank you, toaster'.

BARNEY – STOCKWELL

A mate of mine once sent me a text saying, 'Are you interested in going to a black tie do with your wife?' Unfortunately, he hit the wrong button and sent: 'Are you interested I'm going to a black tie do with your wife?' I was a bit put out.

DAVY IN THE RADAR ROOM

Giving a Sherry Party

This is a popular type of entertainment, as it entails little preparation, and is therefore more suitable for the hostess who has not the staff necessary for giving dinners or more formal gatherings. A sherry party is usually given from about 6 p.m. to 8 p.m., and the hostess sends out an "At Home" card giving the date and time of the party. Often, if it is to be an impromptu or very informal affair, invitations are issued by telephone.

The question of how much sherry to provide is the chief problem. A generous allowance is one bottle for five guests, and let it be said that it is far better to provide too much than to risk running short. It is advisable to buy a certain amount of brown sherry, as some of the guests may prefer it—the ladies especially —and for the rest a dry sherry such as Manzanilla or Amontillado, which should be obtainable for about 4s. 6d. to 5s. a bottle.

Such refreshments as olives, salted almonds, cocktail biscuits, or tiny "bonnes bouches" in the shape of very small and dainty savouries or sandwiches of thin bread and butter rolled round asparagus tips, stuffed celery, etc., are usually offered.

A Cocktail Party is a rather more expensive form of entertaining, and one that needs more preparation, as most cocktails need careful mixing and a number of ingredients are required. It is impossible to give quantities required until it is decided what varieties are to be served, but there are books obtainable which give recipes and quantities for a number of different cocktails. Gin and vermouth (French and Italian), with a little orange juice and a dash of Cointreau is one of the most popular recipes, and others usually met with are Manhattans, Martinis, Sidecars, and White Ladies. Usually it is sufficient to serve two or at the most three different varieties.

How to handle a bear cub

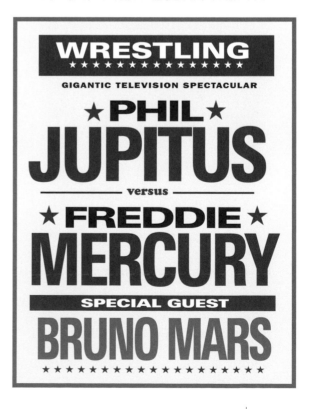

WRESTLING
★★★★★★★★★★★★★★★★★

GIGANTIC TELEVISION SPECTACULAR

★ **PHIL** ★
JUPITUS

versus

★ **FREDDIE** ★
MERCURY

SPECIAL GUEST

BRUNO MARS
★★★★★★★★★★★★★★★★★

Some years ago, after a night of general chat, a friend and I were walking from another friend's house to my own in the leafy suburb of Brockley in south-east London. I had drunk only tea or soft drinks all night and had consumed no drugs whatsoever. It was around 6 a.m. and dawn was breaking when we saw a figure walking up the street towards us. The word we coined later to describe its movement was 'lolloping'– a kind of up and down bouncy walk. It took a few seconds for the two of us to realize this was no human being.

'See that man?' I asked.

'Yes.'

'It's not a man, though, is it?' I found myself saying.

'No,' said my mate, sounding scared. 'It isn't.'

The creature was entirely black and like a cardboard cutout, flat and one-dimensional. It had no features at all, and arms that hung down to its knees. It seemed to be ignoring us, then suddenly seemed to realize we could see it and began to 'lollop' faster towards us. We ran to my front door and hid in the hallway as quiet and unmoving as possible when we saw the thing – we felt it was male – approach the front door and appear to look through the glass from the way its head moved up and down and around. It then turned away.

We didn't sleep for some time after that, discussing what we saw. It was shaped like many descriptions of 'greys', but both of us came away with the impression that what we saw was not of this world but a parallel dimension. We instinctively felt it was not a creature to try and communicate with, and not something that it was good to be near. We felt that if this creature had somehow got hold of us, we would not be around to tell the tale.

A H-H By email to Fortean Times 2005

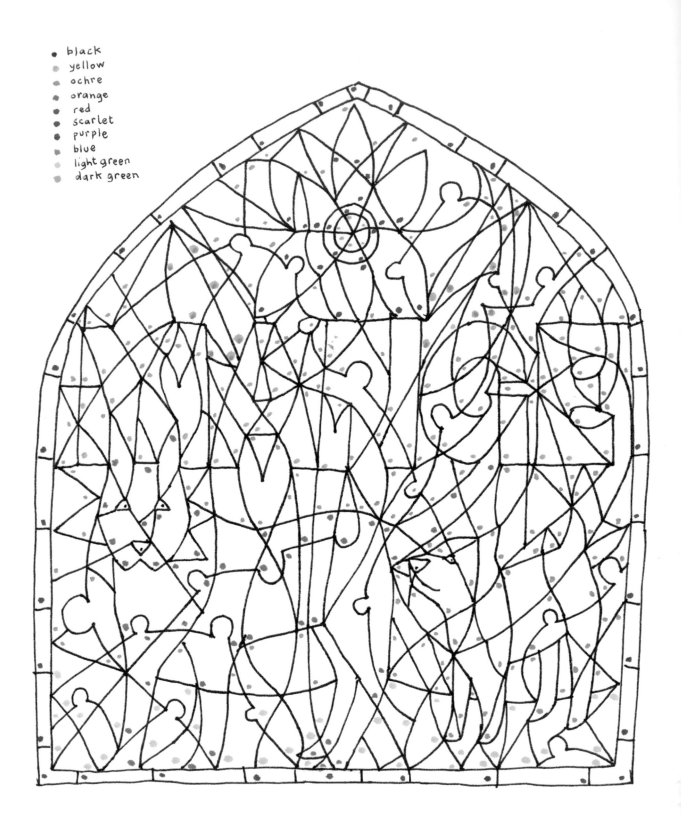

- black
- yellow
- ochre
- orange
- red
- scarlet
- purple
- blue
- light green
- dark green

1960/1 Poetry in Motion Johnny Tillotson

Rock n Roll-y
a gentle enough opener, familiar sing-a-long
lots to enjoy from production to diction!

1959 It's Late Ricky Nelson

well recorded & punchy, is he a rockabilly? polished act
Ricky N. Showbiz family... his 'Garden Party' was the song
dad used to finish his act when
I was little.

73 Sorrow David Bowie

from Pin ups covers album... I ♡ this...
also by/
covered by The McCoys in '65 & The Merseys '66
(folky)   (upbeat)

The Way You Make Me Feel Paul Anka

from Rock Swings Album who better to give a "standards"
version - tongue in cheek, Paul Anka wrote "She's a Lady"
& "it doesn't matter anymore" Tom Jones

Ship of Fools World Party
Buddy Holly

Karl Wallinger is world party, a one man band
I think he's fantastic

1998 Hundreds of Sparrows Sparklehorse

he wrote "She's the One"
Robbie Williams' big song

1971 I Feel the Earth Move Carole King
opening track of the mighty 'Tapestry'

described as "hippie-chick eroticism" she's every
woman

1964 Lucky, Lucky Me Marvin Gaye
Carole

great drive he's so easy to listen to, good track

1963 Little Red Rooster Sam Cooke
I love Sam C's voice so much, this is (organ aside!)
my fave version of this song...

time for a
Leonard C track,
avoiding the obvious
Nevermind Leonard Cohen
Dark, brooding change of pace...
moderns it all
up he grabs your
attention Leonard.

67? The Tears of a Clown Smokey and the Miracles

hit in 1970 in the UK. Classic, Stevie Wonder, Smokey & Hank Cosby wrote it,
good BASSOONING

Until You Come Back To Me Aretha →

stevie w collaborated on this too, from one astonishing singer 6
another

Something Shirley Bassey ←
this song led to a big re-evaluation of Shirley
her talent & her class... fantastic live & Ive

short
for
nd o
hour
needs
1961 I've Told Every Little Star Linda Scott
always thought her
Gold disc for Linda, she was still
one of the best dressed
at school when she did
acts Ive ever
this.
seen

1956 Tonight You Belong To Me Patience & Prudence

original was 1926
Sisters, their dad was
an orchestra leader...

either ending would be pleasing, & I
ger to save one for another day

Without looking them up, how many places can you peg on the map?

Dundee
Ayr
Durham
Stratford-upon-Avon
Plymouth
Ipswich
Londonderry
Chichester
Great Yarmouth
Tralee

Penrith
Fishguard
Sheffield
Bournemouth
Zennor
Skegness
Ullapool
Oxford
Yell

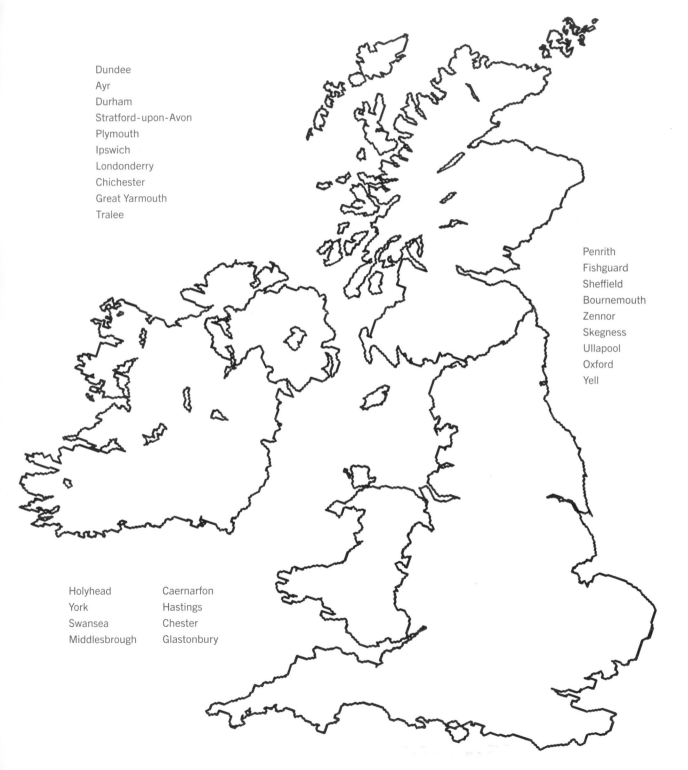

Holyhead   Caernarfon
York   Hastings
Swansea   Chester
Middlesbrough Glastonbury

Some of my favourite Barbie clothes that I hoarded
and wouldn't give to my cousins

or my niece

or bin it

* and girls

what the hell's this about? more facile guff about crap you never needed. snexxed up by advert specialists in a cloak & their stinking design. oh girls how they've USED us...

Gambling has enfuriate me, designed to entrap adolescent boys & pumped into my home willy nilly. The fun's stopped you heartless business people your moral code is in tatters.

I am every shouting woman in a bank. about their business in spite of it.

The other day, whilst travelling home, I overheard a lady say to her male companion, 'If you don't stop winding me up I swear I will go out and buy a violin'. I've never heard that used as a deterrent.

MARIAN – MANCHESTER

In the late 1950s, an elderly nun took my class of nine-year-olds to see 'South Pacific'. She thought it was a geography film.

HILARY – GLOUCESTER

My Labrador spotted some lovers lying in the grass in a local park and jumped on them. He then stole the guy's wallet. When he realized he was the centre of attention, he jumped into the river with it!

PAULA – DERBY

Crepuscular refers to animals active at dawn and dusk. Also to rays of sunlight beaming down from around clouds, often seen at twilight. Good, eh?

DAVID – BATH

I went to see my daughter in her school play. Another girl was the main part and I was sitting next to her mum. After the show I turned to her mum and got fuddled in my head. I wanted to say her daughter was awesome/wonderful. I ended up saying that I thought she was awful!

PHILLIS – LEWES

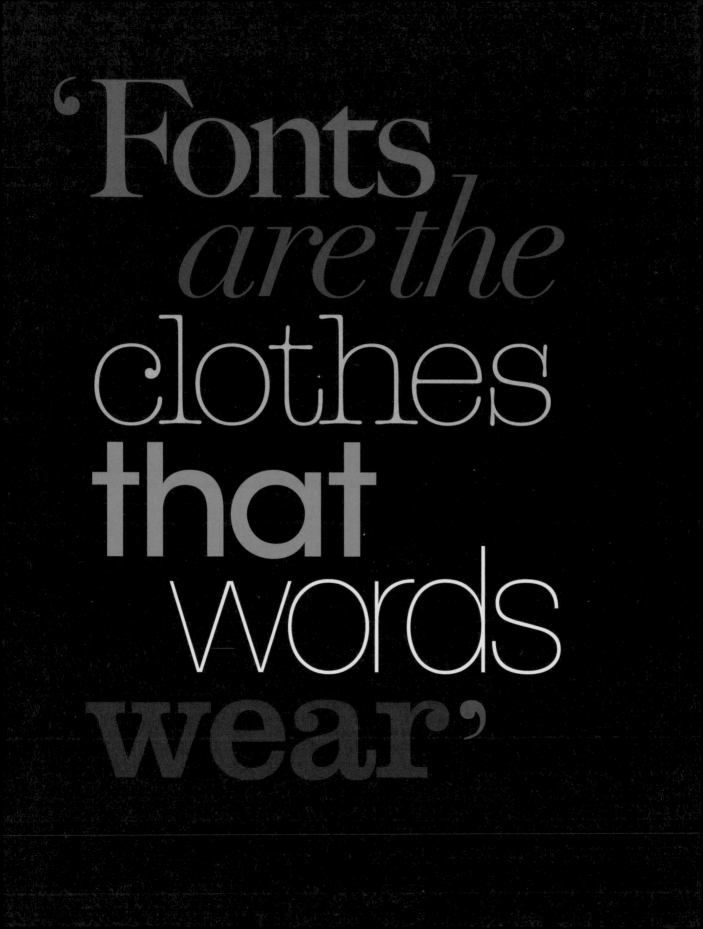

'Fonts *are the* clothes that words wear'

Spat the Deference

Can you spot the twenty-one differences between these two pictures?

There are twelve people in this photo — can you name nine of them?

VICTORIA WOOD

I grew up in genteel Cheltenham. My mum and I would often walk to the local shops which meant going past a public loo with 'MUFC' graffitied on the outside wall. When I asked my mum what it meant she would always say she didn't know, which I took to mean it was too rude to tell me. It was only many years later that I realized it meant Manchester United Football Club.

VERITY – CHELTENHAM

I once went into a supermarket and asked a young man stacking the shelves if he could point me in the direction of pearl barley. He thought for a minute and said he didn't think she was working today.

JANE & DARRELL – BROADSTAIRS

To get a Welsh accent try saying antibiotic. It works every time.

THE MATTHEWS FAMILY

I suffer from nightmares a lot and I scream in my sleep. I'm often woken from them by my GAWJUS husband and knight in shining armour, Martyn. There was one memorable nightmare that chilled me to the bone. I dreamt that I came downstairs and noticed the back door was wide open, so I started panicking thinking it was a burglar. I slowly crept towards the kitchen to find Dale Winton cutting chips. It was terrifying!

VICTORIA – STOCKTON-ON-TEES

BAGUA MAP FOR YOUR HOME

This is a bagua grid in which the various aspects of your life are represented. It is the philosophy of feng shui at its most general, but a very good heads up for any area you may want to pep up or declutter.

WEALTH GOOD LUCK PROSPERITY	FAME REPUTATION	RELATIONSHIPS MARRIAGE
Purples & golds Items that mean prosperity to you Representations of things you're grateful for	FIRE Reds Good lighting candles Triangular shapes	Pinks Things that suggest intimacy to you Pairs of things
FAMILY ANCESTORS YOUR CULTURAL HERITAGE	HEALTH	NEW PROJECTS CREATIVITY CHILDREN
WOOD Greens & Blues Plants Things made of wood Family photos Strong vertical things like a floor lamp.	EARTH Yellows & earth tones Keep this area as clear as possible Earthenware Ceramics Square items	METAL White & pale pastels Things that help you imagine the future Round & oval things, arches Metal objects
BELIEF WISDOM SELF-KNOWLEDGE	VOCATIONS CAREER LIFE PATH	HELPFUL PEOPLE ANGELS TRAVEL
Dark greens & blues Books A place to read or study Comfy chair	WATER Dark colours, blacks Pictures of water, mirrors, glass Floaty fabrics A water feature	Greys & pastels Travel souvenirs, maps Symbols or pictures of people you'd like in your life People who you've made a difference to

ALIGN ENTRANCE TO YOUR HOME ALONG THIS LINE

Draw a rough floorplan of your home and divide it into nine as shown in the grid.

Some areas may be incomplete or missing, so these are the places that need a boost. There may be areas of your life that you can improve by swapping a picture or moving a light. You don't have to apply all of the suggested enhancements, but if something's easy to switch, it's worth a go, isn't it?

It's the power of your intention that really matters.

Vehicles I'd like to drive

Things that you do once and never do again
Stay in a hotel room near the lift
Live in a basement flat
Give the benefit of the doubt to a wet kisser

JOHN MASEFIELD
Poet, dramatist, and novelist, John Edward Masefield was first widely acclaimed in 1911 on the appearance of his narrative poem, " The Everlasting Mercy." He became Poet Laureate in 1930.

Sorry I missed you when I came to ~~deliver~~ parcel(s)

Name:
Date:
D D / M M   Time: H H : M M
I have left your parcel in a safe location as requested by the sender   IN BUSH
I have left your parcel with a neighbour at:
Your parcel is now with
/ your advised safe place
ur for your parcel.
ddress only and

Ten advert jingles
from your youth
you can
still sing...  GO

Cockington

1969   11
"I suppose from now on I'll have to feel guilty when I kiss another woman."

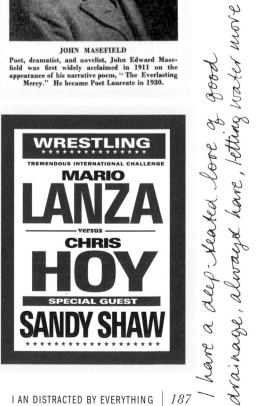
WRESTLING
★★★★★★★
TREMENDOUS INTERNATIONAL CHALLENGE
MARIO LANZA
versus
CHRIS HOY
SPECIAL GUEST
SANDY SHAW
★★★★★★★

People who say " I know " all the time Should know how bloody annoying that is.

I have a deep-seated love of good drainage, always have, letting water move

10 ISLANDS that surround the United Kingdom GO

The Holly.
(Ilex Aquifolium.)
The Holly is usually seen as a small tree in hedgerows and forest glades, though under favourable conditions it sometimes attains 50-70 ft. in height. Its ancient name *Holm* appears in Holmsdale, Holmwood and Holmbury, Surrey, where Hollies still flourish. The spiny, glossy evergreen leaves and brilliant scarlet berries (3) are well-known. Bird-lime is prepared from the smooth, pale-grey bark. The hard, fine-grained wood is valued for inlaid work (2), turnery, musical instruments, teapot-handles (1), etc. It takes stain well, and when dyed black forms a useful substitute for ebony.

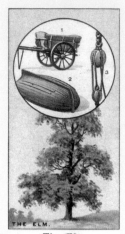

The Elm.
(Ulmus campestris.)
A tree of the hedgerows and woods, less common in Scotland than in England. Its average height is 70-80 ft., though under favourable conditions Elms sometimes attain 130 ft. or even more. The small flowers appear in March and April before the leaves, and are succeeded by winged seeds. Elms are usually propagated by root-suckers or by layering. The close-grained brown wood was formerly in demand for water-pipes and for piles for bridges (e.g. Old London Bridge). It is used for keels (2) and other timbers of boats and ships, blocks for rigging (3), coffins, wheels and cart-planking (1).

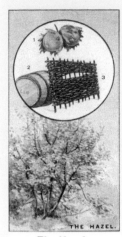

The Hazel.
(Corylus Avellana.)
Usually a shrub of woods and hedgerows, about 12 ft. high, the Hazel when left alone develops into a small tree some 30 ft. in height. The yellow catkins appear in Feb. and Mar., before the leaves. These are of a purplish tint at first, becoming greener in summer and changing in autumn to brown and rich yellow. The pliant branches provide hoops for barrels and crates (2); walking-sticks, and hurdles (3). The larger wood is a source of charcoal, and the roots yield veneers for cabinet-work. Cob-nuts, Filberts and Barcelona-nuts are well-known varieties of the Hazel.

The Alder.
(Alnus glutinosa.)
A tree of the riverside, usually some 40 ft. in height, attaining under favourable conditions 60-70 ft. Its short-stalked leaves remain green after other trees have assumed the reds and yellows of autumn, and are shed later than those of trees in drier situations. The reddish catkins are succeeded by the cones, which ripen in Oct. and Nov. Alder-wood is soft, white when newly-cut, changing to pale red. Being durable under water, it is used for piles (3), the supports of the Rialto at Venice being of this wood. Lasts, clogs (2), turnery, herring-casks (1), and ply-veneers are also made of alder.

The Walnut.
(Juglans regia.)
A native of the Himalayas and of Asia Minor and Greece, the Walnut has been cultivated in Britain since the 15th cent. It is a handsome tree, some 40-60 ft. high, with a bole 20 ft. in circumference, and bearing a profusion of large, fragrant leaves. In the familiar plum-like fruit, the green flesh becomes brown and splits revealing the "stone" or Walnut. When young the fruits are used for pickling, while the ripe Walnuts are much appreciated for dessert (1 and 2). The tough finely-figured wood, easily worked and capable of a beautiful polish, is used for furniture (3) and gun-stocks (4).

The Lime.
(Tilia europaea.)
Three species of Lime or Linden are in cultivation — the Small-leaved, the Large-leaved, and the Intermediate or Common Lime. Under favourable conditions the Large-leaved species attains a height of some 90 ft. It is clothed in spring with leaves of delicate transparent green, and in summer its fragrant flowers, rich in honey, attract bees innumerable. The light, white, fine-grained wood is used by turners and carvers (1), many famous works of Grinling Gibbons having been executed in Lime. This wood is also used in pianofortes and harps (2), and for cricket-bats and malt shovels (3).

The Sycamore.
(Acer pseudo-platanus.)
Unlike the Common Maple, the Sycamore or Great Maple is not a native, having been introduced from the Continent about the 15th century. It is a handsome tree growing to 60-80 ft., and bearing long clusters of bloom succeeded by bunches of red-brown "keys"—winged fruits about 1½ ins. long. The close, tough wood is used by turners for bowls, cups, pattern-blocks, rollers of mangles and washing machines (2), moulds (3), and platters (1). Makers of furniture employ it in its natural state, and also stained to a beautiful silver-grey when it is termed "Artificial Harewood."

The Apple.
(Pyrus malus.)
The Wild Apple tree, though often attaining a height of 20 to 30 ft., is sometimes little larger than a good-sized bush. In May its crooked spreading branches bear an abundance of fragrant blossoms, replaced in autumn by miniature apples of yellow and red. Cider and jelly are made from these, also a vinegar known as *verjuice*. Cultivated apples are of three classes: dessert (1), culinary and cider apples (2). Herefordshire and Devonshire are centres of cultivation, where cider manufacture is an important industry. Apple wood, which is reddish-brown in colour, is used for cog-wheels (3) and turnery.

DRESS UP SHIRLEY

foam hand

loud hailer

paper & comb

Palace outfit

panto Dame wig

Welsh bonnet

D.B.E.

selfie stick

Twister

Glasto wellies

rarebit

Dame Shirley cocktail

carp

GENE HACKMAN

♡ ♡ ♡ ♡ at ente Sailor

I was watching a woman on a survival programme repeatedly saying 'I can't do it, I CAN'T do it'. It was like she was trying the words out and the sound of them was a kind of solution – if she said them enough times she'd get herself out of there and back home.

Actually all they did was put her into a self-paralysing limbo.

One good talking-to from her camp buddy and she was back on track, but listening to the 'I can't' thing was interesting.

You can't argue for 'I can't' because you don't really mean it, it's profoundly not true.

I think 'I can't' is just another way of saying 'help me' or 'I'm scared'.

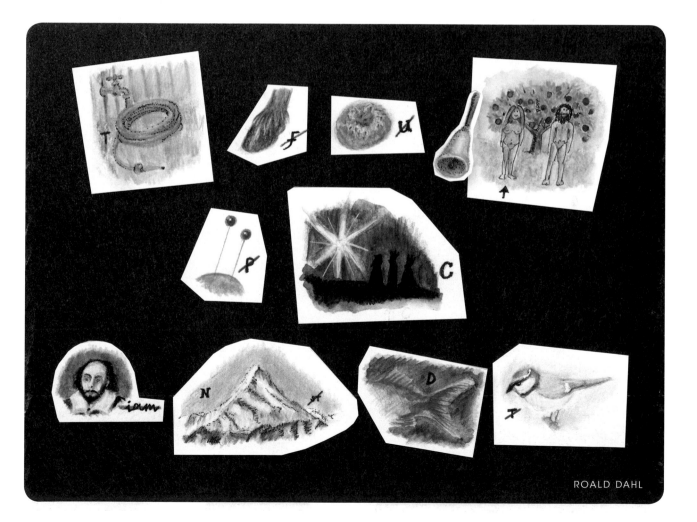

ROALD DAHL

After a day gardening, I was lounging on the sofa. My husband was sitting in an armchair nearby. Something came on the telly, which I commented on. He didn't respond so I flung my arm out and tapped the arm of his chair. The cat sitting on the arm of the chair leapt into Hubby's lap. As Hubby was wearing shorts, he screamed in pain and the cat leapt onto his head, where he sat like a Davy Crockett's hat. It was some hours before we stopped all the bleeding.

LINDA

Whenever I hang out the washing, I have to hang out the socks in pairs so that they don't feel lonely.

LYNDY – WEST SUSSEX

As a child I took part in a market research survey comparing two trifles. I had to eat both, and then say which I liked better. I didn't want to choose one in case the other felt sad. I wouldn't say why I couldn't choose. The woman got really cross with me.

ZOE – HALE, CHESHIRE

When my brother was around five years old the hairdresser asked what his daddy did for a living. He said, 'Well he hasn't got a proper job like a milkman or a postman'. My dad was and still is a financial advisor.

SOPHIE – HARROGATE

Sex Urge Killed Hundreds

MEN and women have been known to die through unrequited love. But at least the member of the opposite sex with whom they were so fatally infatuated was a human being too. In the parish church at Dalham, near Newmarket, however, sex-starved death watch beetles were lured to their doom not by one of their own species, but by a mere mechanical gadget.

It came about after the vicar, the Reverend Hugh Cartwright, found that the beetles were infesting the ancient timber and doing frightful damage. Knowing that to destroy the pests by chemicals would be a highly expensive job, he asked Dr. Harry Hurst, a scientist, if he could help. Dr. Hurst could and did, and in a highly ingenious and yet simple way. He recorded the beetle's mating call on tape, and broadcast it continuously over four loud speakers both day and night. The results were amazing. Excited by the recording, the beetles responded as the doctor hoped they would. They gave the genuine mating call in reply, a rhythmic tapping made by knocking their heads on the wood.

This was their downfall. As the recording went on and on without a break the beetles became more and more frustrated and agitated. And so in desperation they kept banging their heads harder and harder until they knocked themselves unconscious. Then they fell to the floor in their hundreds, and were quickly despatched.

Highly satisfactory, as Dr. Hurst agreed. But as he pointed out: "The mating call is an inescapable stimulus—like drug addiction!" Adding drily: "Teenage girls respond to the Beatles in almost exactly the same way. They scream and shout. You just can't help noticing the similarities!"

Not a statement which will exactly endear Dr. Hurst to the pop fans!

ON A MODEL RAILWAY.

A. BISHOP.

A CONSCIOUS

Nothing Like PHOSFERINE for Perfect Health

Mr. A. J. CHAPMAN *writes* :—

"I BUILT my own house and am now engaged upon the erection of a bungalow and the construction of a large swimming pool. I often work from 12 to 14 hours a day and am then loath to knock off. To stand the strain of such work in all kinds of weather, perfect health and physical fitness is essential, and it is to Phosferine that I owe much of the state of my health. I am now never without this excellent tonic. I find it invaluable for all nerve pains and for warding off chills and colds, and for keeping fatigue at bay there is nothing like Phosferine. You can publish this letter if you wish, as I think other men ought to know and profit by my experience." (" *Upatree,*" *Barkham Ride, Finchampstead, Berks.* 16th July, 1926.)

From the very first day you take PHOSFERINE you will gain new confidence, new life, new endurance. It makes you eat better and sleep better, and you will look as fit as you feel. Phosferine is given with equally good results to the children.

PHOSFERINE

THE GREATEST OF ALL TONICS FOR

Influenza	Neuralgia	Lassitude	Nerve Shock
Debility	Maternity Weakness	Neuritis	Malaria
Indigestion	Weak Digestion	Faintness	Rheumatism
Sleeplessness	Mental Exhaustion	Brain Fag	Headache
Exhaustion	Loss of Appetite	Anæmia	Sciatica

WRESTLING
SENSATIONAL MAIN EVENT
JOHN PARROTT
versus
WALTER PIDGEON
SPECIAL GUEST
GREGORY PECK

Lon Chaney in *London After Midnight* (1927)

'I want to be the person my dog thinks I am.'

On the way to London Bridge (not sure if it is still there – graffiti not bridge!) for years we saw 'Big Dave's Gusset'. Who was Dave? And what was so special about his gusset? Loved it and still love it. Everyone I know who took that route into London saw it and I know there are loads of us that still laugh about it now. I won't even mention the 'I feel like Alan Minter' on the wall before Blackheath!

MEL & STEVE – ROCHESTER

If the lady who just dropped her glasses down the loo thinks she's got problems, I've just coated the inside of my oven with furniture polish instead of oven cleaner. Similar looking cans are an annoyance, aren't they?

SYMEON – NORTHAMPTON

My cat Tiggy used to come home every Sunday morning with a 'still warm' sausage in her jaws. We never knew where she got it from.

ELLA

Just outside Chippenham there is a village called Easton and it always makes me laugh when I drive past because someone has written 'Sheena' above it. DENISE

An Afternoon with Alice

Alice has decided to open her own tea shop and in Wonderland chaos predictably ensues. There is no point in trying to rationalize the meaning or logic in the hidden items other than their appearance in the original stories, just try and have fun in finding them. There are 16 altogether.

THE LAUGHING HEART

your life is your life
don't let it be clubbed into dank submission.
be on the watch.
there are ways out.
there is a light somewhere.
it may not be much light but
it beats the darkness.
be on the watch.
the gods will offer you chances.
know them.
take them.
you can't beat death but
you can beat death in life, sometimes.
and the more often you learn to do it,
the more light there will be.
your life is your life.
know it while you have it.
you are marvelous
the gods wait to delight
in you.

Charles Bukowski

My effervescent thanks to:

Jonathan Whitelocke, Sarah Godsill, the best agent in London – Debi Allen, Cathal Joseph Smyth, Lisa 'Darkus' Clarke, Babette Lee, Stewart Martin Johnson, Jillian Taylor, Louise Moore, Catriona Hillerton, Kevin Robinson, Sue Vincent, Tom Stuart, Maff Taylor, Cheryl Tarbuck, Jimmy Tarbuck, Pauline Tarbuck, Dr Masaru Emoto, Nathanael Sherwood, Phillippa, Dom with the Phoenician dad, David Cotsworth the brilliant photographer, Sarah Hughes, Lynn Osborne, Jessica Rickson, Marco Beneden, Victoria Wood, Fiona Day, Kylie's shorts, Pip Worlidge, Charlene Nelmes, Tattia Lasa Tarbuck, Rosie Harrison, Oscar and Louis Lasa, Basia Barbara, Helen Monks, Karl Parker, Dylan Hearne, Dawn French, Linda Kay, Lotty Williams, Jess Molloy, Susan Purrrkins, Ed Forsdick, Cody Lunstrum, Betty Monk, Loretta Dives, did I say Pauline and Jimmy? – they're really bloody fabulous, the listeners who feel compelled to get in touch of a Saturday, Stephanie Tralls, my R2 gang, music fans, Barry, Steve Wright, Wilfred Tarbuck, Vorny, Phil Edgar-Jones, Helen Simpson, that bloke from AltJ, David Bowie, Peter Blake, Tim and Lesley, my sparrows, Terry Jones, Bernard Carfoot, other unknown forces, Jason Hazeley, Holly Robinson, Luke the filthy boozer, Elizabeth Groper, all the children who keep me childlike & the inspiring people who wander around every day exuding curiosity and openness.

I couldn't have done it if Debi didn't keep remembering things I'd said, if Louise Moore hadn't trusted me, if Jillian Taylor hadn't unlocked me with A3 paper, if Cathal Smashing hadn't been such a magnificent friend, if Lisa Clarke wasn't so clever, if Jon Whitelocke hadn't 'got me' from the start and welcomed my intrusions, if Sarah Godsill hadn't been my friend for forty-seven years . . . thank you, thanky thanky thank YOU.

'I'd like to say thank you on behalf of the group and ourselves and I hope we've passed the audition'. JL